VOLUME 4

The Books of the Prophets

CONCORDIA PUBLISHING HOUSE · SAINT LOUIS

3558 S. Jefferson Ave., St. Louis, MO 63118-3968
1-800-325-3040 • cph.org

Illustrations by Dede Putra

Portions of this book have been compiled from, adapted from, and inspired by various sources, including *The Lutheran Study Bible*, Concordia Publishing House, 2009; the Concordia Commentary series, Concordia Publishing House, 1996–; *Lutheran Bible Companion*, vol. 1, Concordia Publishing House, 2014; and *Concordia's Complete Bible Handbook for Students*, Concordia Publishing House, 2011.

Manufactured in China

Library of Congress Cataloging-in-Publication Data

Title: The Books of the Prophets: guiding word.

Description: Saint Louis : Concordia Publishing House, 2024- | Series: The guiding word ; volume 4 | Summary: "This six-volume series will take readers through each book of the Bible, showing the unified narrative of God's plan of salvation. Using this resource, readers will (1) understand the history of God's people and His promise; (2) gain a basic grasp of each book of the Bible; (3) see Jesus' saving mission in each book of the Bible; and (4) develop fundamental Bible reading and interpretation skills"-- Provided by publisher.

Identifiers: LCCN 2022060172 (print) | LCCN 2022060173 (ebook) | ISBN 9780758671943 (v. 4 ; paperback) | ISBN 9780758671950 (v. 4 ; ebook)

Subjects: LCSH: Bible Old Testament--Introductions.

Classification: LCC BS1140.3 .B66 2024 (print) | LCC BS1140.3 (ebook) | DDC 221.6--dc23/eng/20230621

LC record available at https://lccn.loc.gov/2022060172

LC ebook record available at https://lccn.loc.gov/2022060173

---

1 2 3 4 5 6 7 8 9 10 34 33 32 31 30 29 28 27 26 25

TABLE OF CONTENTS

Welcome

Welcome to *Guiding Word*. This six-volume collection will help you better read and understand the Bible, the most important book ever written. In it, we read and hear God's Word, which is written so that we may believe that Jesus is the Christ, and that by believing we may have eternal life in His name (John 20:31).

Why have another Bible resource? First, the Bible is a complex library of books, and it is often intimidating for people to read on their own. Second, while there are many resources designed to help you read and understand the Bible, each has its own format and style and may not be suitable for every learner. We hope this resource will fill a gap and be useful for you.

Think of this series of books as a travel guide to the Bible. Just as a travel guide helps you prepare for and better enjoy a trip, this resource will enable you to better understand and appreciate the Bible as you journey through it. The sections have been designed to help you prepare for reading and understanding difficult passages, to explain the overall course of the Scriptures, to prompt you to reflect on the text as you read, to point out important milestones and events, and to guide you to Jesus' presence throughout the Bible.

If you are already familiar with the organization of the Bible, feel free to skip ahead to the section titled "What's in *Guiding Word*?"

What's in the Bible?

The Bible is all about God's plan to restore fallen humanity and His broken creation by sending His Son. But what's in the Bible? How do we look at it? How do we use it? Though we call the Bible a book, it's actually a collection of sixty-six books. These were written over a period of 1,500 years by many authors.

The Bible has two divisions: the Old Testament and the New Testament. We don't use the word *testament* too often today. It's related to words like *covenant* and *contract*.

The Old Testament includes the first thirty-nine books of the Bible. These are the books written about the events that happened before Jesus was born. They all point us toward Jesus. The name *Old Testament* is a little misleading because sometimes we think of old things as not important or out of style. Instead, these books can be thought of as the first covenant or promise that God made to His people to send the Savior, Jesus. And as you will see, Jesus is present throughout the Old Testament. The New Testament includes the last twenty-seven books of the Bible, which record Jesus' life and mission, as well as the life of Jesus' early followers in the church. These books point us back to Jesus and how He fulfilled all of God's promises made for us in the Old Testament. Again, these are all about Jesus.

The books of the Bible are organized in a way that may seem confusing at first but makes sense when you know the system. How are the books in a library organized? In libraries, books are organized by their type. Fiction is in one section, and nonfiction is in another; magazines are in one spot and children's books in another. The same goes for the Bible. Instead of the books being ordered by the date they were written or by their authors, the books of the Bible are put in categories, or genres; then the books are generally organized by date written within that genre.

Navigating the Library

The first five books of the Old Testament—Genesis, Exodus, Leviticus, Numbers, and Deuteronomy—are called the Books of Moses, or the Torah, meaning "Law of God." They were written down by Moses and are covered in the first volume of this series.

The next books in the Old Testament are called the Books of History. These tell the history of God's people from the time of Moses up to the time of Jesus and are covered in the second volume.

Next are the Books of Wisdom and Poetry. These poetical books were written at different times during the Old Testament history, mostly by kings David and Solomon. These are covered in the third volume.

The last group of Old Testament books are the Books of the Prophets. These books record God's special messages to His Old Testament people, mostly during the second half of their history. They are discussed in the fourth volume.

The New Testament has five genres. The first four books—Matthew, Mark, Luke, and John—are called the Gospels. Each Gospel tells of the life and mission of Jesus from a different writer and perspective. These accounts make up the heart of the Bible and are covered in the fifth *Guiding Word* volume.

Next is the book of the Acts of the Apostles (also known simply as Acts). This historical book records events from the early years of the Christian Church and the lives of the first Christians after Jesus ascended into heaven. The next books are called the Pauline Epistles (*epistle* means "letter"). These are letters that the apostle Paul wrote to the early Christians. Near the end of the New Testament are the General Epistles. These are letters that other people besides Paul wrote to the early Christians. The final book of the Bible is the only book of prophecy in the New Testament, the book of Revelation. This shows the vision Jesus revealed to the apostle John about life in the end times (that is, the time between Christ's first and second coming) and the restoration of God's creation. The books of Acts through Revelation are covered in the sixth and final volume of *Guiding Word.*

66 BOOKS OF THE BIBLE

	Category	Books
OLD TESTAMENT	BOOKS OF MOSES *(Torah)*	GENESIS, EXODUS, LEVITICUS, NUMBERS, DEUTERONOMY
	HISTORY	JOSHUA, JUDGES, RUTH, 1 SAMUEL, 2 SAMUEL, 1 KINGS, 2 KINGS, 1 CHRONICLES, 2 CHRONICLES, EZRA, NEHEMIAH, ESTHER
	WISDOM & POETRY	JOB, PSALMS, PROVERBS, ECCLESIASTES, SONG OF SOLOMON
	PROPHETS	ISAIAH, JEREMIAH, LAMENTATIONS, EZEKIEL, DANIEL, HOSEA, JOEL, AMOS, OBADIAH, JONAH, MICAH, NAHUM, HABAKKUK, ZEPHANIAH, HAGGAI, ZECHARIAH, MALACHI
NEW TESTAMENT	GOSPELS	MATTHEW, MARK, LUKE, JOHN
	HISTORY	ACTS
	PAULINE EPISTLES *(Letters)*	ROMANS, 1 CORINTHIANS, 2 CORINTHIANS, GALATIANS, EPHESIANS, PHILIPPIANS, COLOSSIANS, 1 THESSALONIANS, 2 THESSALONIANS, 1 TIMOTHY, 2 TIMOTHY, TITUS, PHILEMON
	GENERAL EPISTLES	HEBREWS, JAMES, 1 PETER, 2 PETER, 1 JOHN, 2 JOHN, 3 JOHN, JUDE
	END TIMES	REVELATION

Navigating the Bible

When you open up a Bible, you'll see chapter and verse numbers scattered throughout the pages. Did you know that those numbers were not originally there? As people used the Bible more and more and made copies, later scholars eventually put in these numbers to help people quickly find sections or passages. We call these Bible references.

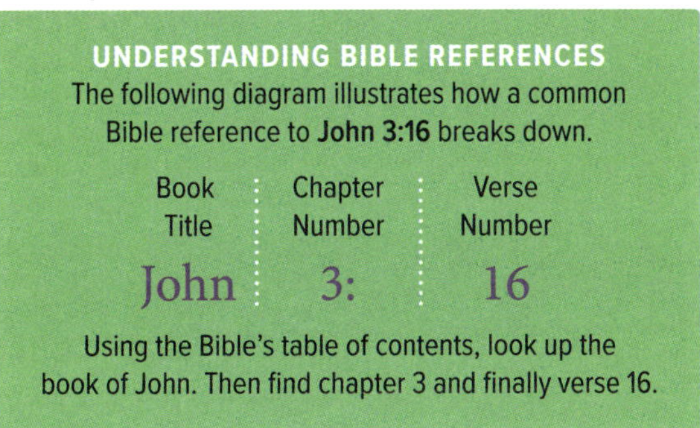

What's in *Guiding Word*?

Each volume of *Guiding Word* is laid out in a similar fashion. After this series introduction is an introduction for that specific volume. Then, each book of the Bible has its own introduction, which will help you better understand and dig into that particular book.

Each book of the Bible follows an outline, which breaks the book into major divisions and then each division into sections. The section heads were not included in the original biblical text but were added later to help clarify how the text flows from narrative to narrative or idea to idea. In *Guiding Word*, these correspond to the subheadings in the ESV translation of the Bible. From here on out, we will refer to these subhead sections as "passages."

Following the pattern of a travel guide, *Guiding Word* includes some features to help you read through, better understand, and reflect on each passage of the Bible. These features include the following:

(1) **Orientation.** This is a short summary of each passage. Just as a travel guide gives you a glimpse of where you will be going on your journey before you arrive, the summary will help orient you to where you are in the Bible and where you are going. After reading the summary for each passage, read the text itself in your Bible. Alternatively, if you are skimming a book of the Bible, previewing the book, or only want to understand the high points before reading deeper, these summaries are a good place to start.

(2) **Observation Points.** In the side margins, you will find open-ended questions. Use these reflection questions to help you slow down, observe, and reflect on the passage. There is room in the side margin for recording reflections, thoughts, and notes as you go. Just as a travel guide will prompt you to look out for specific things on your way, the reflection questions will help you better observe what's going on in the text.

(3) **Landmarks.** These special features, interspersed in the text, will help you appreciate the overall journey through God's Word. In any journey, you will encounter landmarks of all types that pop out to you, may interest you, or may even make you scratch your head. Landmarks in *Guiding Word* are identified by icons and colored bars, and can be read before or after you read the corresponding passage. Landmarks include the following categories:

VISUALIZE

This feature includes maps, diagrams, pictures, or infographics to help you visualize scenes, locations, and concepts in a passage.

PICTURE OF THE SAVIOR

This Old Testament feature highlights people, places, or events that set the stage for the coming of Jesus and help reveal His work of salvation.

LINK BETWEEN THE TESTAMENTS

In the Old Testament, this highlights people or events that Jesus or His apostles will discuss, explain, or fulfill in the New Testament. In the New Testament, this feature points the reader back to the Old Testament person or event that set the stage for the New Testament passage.

CLEAR THE CONFUSION

This Landmark clarifies passages that are likely to leave the reader confused and fills the gaps—providing backstories, describing future developments, or discussing the significance of the event.

SET THE SCENE

This feature explains important cultural or historical themes that help you better understand the context of the passage.

WAYPOINT

This feature is designed to be a longer stopping point. When you travel, you will likely stop at notable locations for an extended period of time to really experience the destination. Waypoints in *Guiding Word* function like stopping points that are worth investigating along the journey through God's Word. Each Waypoint has a three-part structure:

- What does this text show us?
- What does this text reveal about God's plan of salvation?
- What does this text uncover about our identity and calling as God's people today?

Each Waypoint also has reflection questions associated with it. The Waypoints can be considered on your own or in a group study. However you choose to use the Waypoints is up to you, but use the summaries and reflection prompts to help guide you through a deeper reading of the text.

How to Use *Guiding Word*

You can use this resource in multiple ways:

- Read through the Bible on your own, passage by passage. The summary of each passage will help orient you to where the narrative is taking you, and the reflection questions are observation prompts that will help you pay closer attention to what you're reading. The interspersed Landmark features will help you visualize important images or concepts, or understand and connect key themes to the overall story of Scripture.
- Read through the Bible in a small group or Bible study setting. The guided summaries and reflection questions make good prompts if you are reading through the Scriptures as a group, providing some reflections along the way. The Waypoint sections also serve as great places to stop and reflect on key narratives.
- Read a good thirty-thousand-foot summary of the Bible. *Guiding Word* includes summaries of passages, and if you have never read certain books of the Bible or are intimidated by their length, you can take a few minutes to get introduced or oriented to them via summaries and graphics.

Whether or not you've read through all or parts of the Bible before, *Guiding Word* will serve as your companion and guide through the journey.

The Books of the Prophets

The seventeen Old Testament books covered in this fourth volume of *Guiding Word* confront the disobedience of God's people, calling them to repent and return to God before devastating punishment falls. The prophets also point to the coming Messiah and the day of the Lord, when Jesus will return to judge the living and the dead, restore God's creation, and bring us to live in God's glorious presence forever.

Journeying Through the Books of the Prophets

Isaiah was written around seven hundred years before Jesus' birth. Isaiah shows us the mission of the Messiah, from His conception and birth to His death and resurrection.

Jeremiah was written about one hundred years after Isaiah. This prophet recounts the disobedience of Judah and its leaders, the devastating destruction of Jerusalem, and the exile of God's people to Babylon.

Lamentations was written after Jerusalem's destruction. In the midst of the desolation, Jeremiah points to God's steadfast love and promise of the Messiah, giving His people hope, comfort, and consolation.

Ezekiel wrote to Judah's exiles living in captivity in Babylon. He first attacks the idea that the exiles would soon return to Jerusalem. After the temple is destroyed, Ezekiel promises God will bring them home.

Daniel powerfully shows that God rules all the nations of the earth for the benefit of His people. God does this even with rulers who neither know nor acknowledge Him.

Hosea uses the metaphor of marriage to expose Israel's unfaithfulness and highlight God's love. Through Hosea, we see the length God is willing to go to confront His people in their sin and to call them back to Him in tender love.

Joel uses an invasion of locusts to warn Judah to repent of their sins before God brings an invading army to punish them.

Amos strongly condemns the prominent people of Israel for oppressing the poor and vulnerable. He calls them to repent before disaster strikes.

Obadiah condemns Edom, a nation that victimized the people of Judah when Babylon attacked. He promises the restoration of Israel, the return from exile, and the coming of God's messianic kingdom.

Jonah is a reluctant prophet who resists God's command to warn Nineveh of God's impending judgment for their cruelty and violence.

Micah warns both Judah and Israel of God's impending judgment because of their wayward practices and sin. He mixes in visions of God's kingdom to come and glimpses of the promised messianic King.

Nahum depicts the sacking of Nineveh, the capital city of Assyria, 150 years after they had repented at Jonah's preaching. Nahum condemns Nineveh for its cruel mistreatment of the prisoners of Israel.

Habakkuk records a dialogue between the prophet and the Lord. The prophet asks where God is when evil people oppress the righteous. The Lord teaches Habakkuk to live by faith and not by sight.

Zephaniah prophesies during the rule of righteous King Josiah. While Josiah restores the temple and proper worship for Judah, Zephaniah calls for spiritual renewal and true repentance.

Haggai works with Zechariah to encourage the returned exiles to trust God and resume rebuilding the temple in Jerusalem.

Zechariah joins Haggai to encourage the rebuilding of the temple. Then he goes on to prophesy many of the messianic events of Holy Week.

Malachi writes ninety years after Haggai and Zechariah to restore the priests and people of Judah who have drifted from proper service at the temple. He also predicts the coming of John the Baptist and Jesus.

The Books of the Prophets, with Their General Divisions

- **Isaiah**
  - Judgment on Judah and Jerusalem (1:1–12:6)
  - Oracles About the Nations (13:1–23:18)
  - Cosmic Judgment (24:1–27:13)
  - Ephraim (Samaria) and Jerusalem (28:1–32:20)
  - The Hinge of the Book (33:1–35:10)
  - Isaiah and Hezekiah (36:1–39:8)
  - Comfort for the Lord's Weary People (40:1–31)
  - The Lord Chooses Israel, His Servant (41:1–42:17)
  - The Redemption of Israel (42:18–44:20)
  - Freedom from Babylon (44:21–48:22)
  - The Suffering Servant and Redeemed Israel (49:1–55:13)
  - Understanding Divine Character (56:1–66:24)
- **Jeremiah**
  - The Call of Jeremiah (1:1–19)
  - Prophecy Against Judah (2:1–35:19)
  - Jeremiah's Suffering and Persecution (36:1–38:28)
  - The Fall of Jerusalem (39:1–45:5)
  - Judgment Against the Nations (46:1–51:64)
  - Historical Appendix (52:1–34)
- **Lamentations**
  - The Misery of Jerusalem (1:1–22)
  - The Lord's Anger (2:1–22)
  - The Lord's Discipline and Mercy (3:1–66)
  - Zion's Punishment (4:1–22)
  - A Plea to the Lord (5:1–22)
- **Ezekiel**
  - Ezekiel's Call (1:1–7:27)
  - God's Glory Abandons the Jerusalem Temple (8:1–11:25)
  - Oracles of Judgment on Israel (12:1–24:27)
  - Oracles Against Other Nations (25:1–32:32)
  - Oracles and Visions of Israel's Restoration (33:1–48:35)
- **Daniel**
  - Judeans Steadfast in Practicing Their Faith (1:1–21)
  - Nebuchadnezzar's Dream (2:1–49)
  - God's Faithful Servants Rescued from Death (3:1–30)
  - Nebuchadnezzar Judged for His Arrogance Against God (4:1–37)
  - Belshazzar Judged for His Arrogance Against God (5:1–31)
  - God's Faithful Servant Rescued from Death (6:1–28)
  - Daniel's Visions (7:1–12:13)

- **Hosea**
  - Hosea's Personal Issues as Prophecies (1:1–3:5)
  - Various Oracles (4:1–14:9)
- **Joel**
  - Catastrophes, Current and Coming (1:1–2:17)
  - The Lord's Response (2:18–3:21)
- **Amos**
  - Proclamation of Judgment (1:1–2:16)
  - Israel's Sins and Refusal to Repent (3:1–6:14)
  - Visions (7:1–9:15)
- **Obadiah**
  - The First Proclamation Against Edom: Humiliation (vv. 1–4)
  - The Second Proclamation Against Edom: Displacement (vv. 5–7)
  - The Third Proclamation Against Edom: Destruction (vv. 8–18)
  - Israel's Restoration and the Kingship of Yahweh (vv. 19–21)
- **Jonah**
  - Jonah Flees the Lord's Calling (1:1–2:10)
  - Jonah Preaches God's Warning and Laments Its Effects (3:1–4:11)
- **Micah**
  - Prophecies of Doom Against Various Cities (1:1–3:12)
  - The Coming of God's Salvation and His Rescue (4:1–5:15)
  - Renewed Prophecies of Doom, Ending with Restoration (6:1–7:20)
- **Nahum**
  - Reminder of the Covenant (1:1–15)
  - The Destruction and Humiliation of Nineveh (2:1–3:19)
- **Habakkuk**
  - The Debate Between Habakkuk and God (1:1–2:5)
  - Woes to the Arrogant (2:6–20)
  - Habakkuk's Psalm of Submission (3:1–19)
- **Zephaniah**
  - Impending Judgment (1:1–3:8)
  - Deliverance, Restoration, and Exaltation of the Righteous (3:9–20)
- **Haggai**
  - The Command to Rebuild the Temple (1:1–15)
  - The Coming Glory of the Temple (2:1–23)

- **Zechariah**
  - Introductory Oracle and "Night Visions" (1:1–6:8)
  - The Coming Peace and Prosperity (6:9–10:12)
  - Holy Week Prophecies (11:1–13:9)
  - Varied Pictures of the Last Day (14:1–21)
- **Malachi**
  - Correction for the Priests (1:1–2:9)
  - The People Must Be Faithful Through Proper Marriage Practice (2:10–3:5)
  - A Call to Return to the Lord in Repentance (3:6–4:6)

ISAIAH

Welcome to Isaiah

Isaiah speaks God's Word to four kings of Judah over a span of fifty years. He prophesies the rise and fall of nations and empires. Many of Isaiah's prophecies focus intensely on the coming Messiah, who would come to Judah some seven hundred years later. In fact, Isaiah's many prophecies about the Messiah have led to the book often being called the "Fifth Gospel." As you read Isaiah, watch him prophesy the breadth of Jesus' life and saving ministry.

As you begin reading this book, what do you already know about Isaiah?

Isaiah at a Glance

- **Start:** Isaiah begins with God uncovering the wickedness of the people of Judah but offering to cleanse and purify them.
- **End:** Isaiah ends with a view of eternal life in the new heavens and new earth.
- **Theme:** Isaiah writes to comfort God's people with the good news of their redemption.
- **Author and Date:** The great prophet Isaiah wrote the prophecies of this book between 740 and 681 BC.
- **Places Visited:** Jerusalem, Israel, Syria, Assyria, and other nations
- **Journey Time:** Isaiah's sixty-six chapters can be read in under four hours.
- **Outline:**
  - Judgment on Judah and Jerusalem (1:1–12:6)
  - Oracles About the Nations (13:1–23:18)
  - Cosmic Judgment (24:1–27:13)
  - Ephraim (Samaria) and Jerusalem (28:1–32:20)
  - The Hinge of the Book (33:1–35:10)
  - Isaiah and Hezekiah (36:1–39:8)
  - Comfort for the Lord's Weary People (40:1–31)
  - The Lord Chooses Israel, His Servant (41:1–42:17)

- The Redemption of Israel (42:18–44:20)
- Freedom from Babylon (44:21–48:22)
- The Suffering Servant and Redeemed Israel (49:1–55:13)
- Understanding Divine Character (56:1–66:24)

Five Top Sights and Spectacles of Isaiah

Isaiah's Temple Vision and Commissioning (6:1–13) Feel the temple foundations shake as the seraphim call out above the Lord's throne.

Immanuel and His Reign (7:14; 9:2–7) Listen to Isaiah speak of Jesus' conception and reign among us as our mighty God and Savior.

The Feast (25:6–9) Come and sample the feast of rich food God is preparing on the mountain where He will swallow up death forever.

The Suffering Servant (52:13–53:12) Stand at the foot of the cross as Isaiah explains how Jesus' sufferings have taken away our sins.

The New Heavens and New Earth (65:17–25) Look upon the new heavens and new earth, which God will create on the Last Day.

Seeing Jesus in Isaiah

Nowhere in the Old Testament is Jesus' picture more clearly drawn than in Isaiah. Through prophecies about His birth and person, His godhood, His public ministry, and His sacrifice as the Suffering Servant, the message of the Messiah is woven throughout Isaiah.

Judgment on Judah and Jerusalem (1:1–12:6)

Chapters 1–5 outline God's judgment against Judah's repeated sins. After Chapter 6, when Isaiah recounts God's call to him, chapters 7–12 prophesy attacks from Israel, Syria, and Assyria.

Introduction (1:1)

Isaiah lists the kings who ruled Judah during his prophetic ministry.

The Wickedness of Judah (1:2–20)

God accuses Judah of sin and rebellion. The people go through the motions when they offer sacrifices but mistreat their neighbors. Those who repent will be saved, while those who reject God will be destroyed.

The Unfaithful City (1:21–31)

Jerusalem has become the center of unfaithfulness by trusting in foreign powers and gods rather than the true God. Yet God declares that one day He will restore Jerusalem and it will be called the faithful city.

The Mountain of the LORD (2:1–5)

Isaiah foresees the New Testament church reaching out to all nations with the Gospel, and he ultimately sees the faithful believers of all times and places gathered in the new creation at Christ's return.

CLEAR THE CONFUSION

What are the "latter days" (v. 2)?

In Old Testament prophecy, the "latter days" referred to the time after the Messiah's first coming to earth, the New Testament era. The "former days" described the Old Testament era, before Christ's first coming.

The Day of the LORD (2:6–22)

God describes His impending wrath against evildoers. This "day of the Lord" points both to temporal wrath against Judah and eternal wrath against all sin on Judgment Day, when Christ returns.

Judgment on Judah and Jerusalem (3:1–4:1)

Judah will face scarcity of food, goods, and men due to the violence and oppression they commit against vulnerable fellow Judeans.

The Branch of the LORD Glorified (4:2–6)

Even though God will punish His people's unfaithfulness, He will send the long-promised Messiah. This Branch, Jesus, will arise in history after Judah collapses. This prophecy also points to Christ's final return.

PICTURE OF THE SAVIOR

The Branch of the Lord

Isaiah sometimes used the image of a branch to refer to the Messiah. When Babylon captured and exiled Judah, David's kingly line was cut down like a tree. Yet, from the stump of David's house, the Christ would sprout like a branch.

Like Isaiah, Jesus drew spiritual meaning from earthly objects such as vineyards, sheep, and mustard seeds. Which of Jesus' parables do you find most memorable?

The Vineyard of the LORD Destroyed (5:1–7)

God had provided everything Israel needed to be just and holy. But when the people are unjust and evil, God has no choice but to lay waste to them like to a vineyard that bears bad grapes.

VISUALIZE

LINK BETWEEN THE TESTAMENTS

The Vineyard of the Lord → The Parable of the Tenants (Isaiah 5:1–7 → Matthew 21:33–41)

Isaiah and Jesus both used vineyard imagery to show God's disappointment when His people became more wicked and oppressive than the nations around them. As a result, God gave His vineyard to the nations to loot and plunder.

Woe to the Wicked (5:8–30)

Isaiah continues to describe the various desolations that will come upon the people of Judah because of their wickedness. The Assyrians will ransack their cities and bring darkness and distress.

Isaiah's Vision of the Lord (6:1–7)

WAYPOINT

What does this text show us?
In a vision in the temple, Isaiah sees God sitting on His throne, surrounded by six-winged angels who call out "Holy, holy, holy." When Isaiah trembles at his unworthiness, God sends an angel to touch his lips with a coal from the altar.

What does this text reveal about God's plan of salvation?
God is with believers, even if our eyes cannot see Him. Just as the angel purified Isaiah's lips, making him fit to speak God's word, Christ forgives all who believe in Him. This purifies us to share His holiness with others.

What does this text uncover about our identity and calling as God's people today?
God desires that we receive the forgiveness He won for us in Christ. This is the great calling we have as redeemed children of Christ as we receive God's gifts through the means of grace—the Word and Sacraments.

How might you see worship in your church differently as a result of this vision?

How do we see elements of this passage echoed in worship today?

What are some ways you can honor God more faithfully in your own life?

Isaiah's Commission from the Lord (6:8–13)

Isaiah volunteers when the Lord asks, "Whom shall I send?" God sends him with a message the people will reject, resulting in their defeat and exile. But God promises the Christ will come from Judah.

CLEAR THE CONFUSION

Did God really want His people's hearts to be dull (v. 10) so they would not repent?

God desires to save, not destroy. He was preparing Isaiah for the Judeans' reaction to his message. Judah would suffer defeat and exile before a remnant would repent and be ready to hear the Gospel of the coming Messiah.

Isaiah Sent to King Ahaz (7:1–9)

King Ahaz is terrified of Israel and Syria. When he refuses to join their alliance, Israel and Syria threaten to attack Jerusalem and replace him. God sends Isaiah to urge Ahaz to trust the Lord and stand firm in faith.

The Sign of Immanuel (7:10–25)

God promises to deliver Ahaz and offers a miraculous sign to reassure him. Ahaz rejects the Lord, so Isaiah promises a sign anyway. The virgin will conceive, and Israel and Syria will fall to Assyria.

PICTURE OF THE SAVIOR

Immanuel

The Hebrew word *Immanuel* means "God with us." Matthew 1:22–23 quotes this prophecy and identifies Jesus as Immanuel and Mary as the virgin. Jesus is the Son of God in human flesh, who fulfilled the Lord's promise of redemption.

What kinds of people or things are we tempted to put our hope and confidence in during this life?

The Coming Assyrian Invasion (8:1–10)

God commands Isaiah to make a sign publicly proclaiming that the capitals of Israel and Syria will be destroyed by the Assyrians. He even has Isaiah use this proclamation as the name of his next son.

CLEAR THE CONFUSION

What are the gentle waters of Shiloah and the waters of the River, mighty and many (vv. 6–8)?

Shiloah symbolizes God's promise to protect Judah and restore the nation. The River refers to Assyria. Since Ahaz rejected God's protection and sought Assyria's help, Assyria destroyed Syria and Israel, then swept through Judah.

Fear God, Wait for the LORD (8:11–22)

After King Ahaz allies Judah with Assyria, Isaiah warns that Assyria will soon turn on Judah and bring about much destruction. Isaiah calls on God's people to trust in His Word and recall His promises.

LINK BETWEEN THE TESTAMENTS

The Rock of Offense and Stumbling (Isaiah 8:14–17 → Matthew 21:42–44; Romans 9:30–33)

God is both a sanctuary and a rock of stumbling. For believers, the rock or mountain serves as a stronghold and sanctuary. For unbelievers, He is the rock that causes stumbling; those who fall are broken upon it. Jesus used this image to warn the Jewish rulers against rejecting Him.

The birth of any child is joyous because of the hope it brings into the world. What hope did Jesus' birth bring to the world?

For to Us a Child Is Born (9:1–7)

The lands of Israel's northernmost tribes will be the first to fall to the Assyrians, yet the Messiah will arise from this place, Galilee of the nations, and His reign will last forever.

Judgment on Arrogance and Oppression (9:8–10:4)

Israel will be destroyed because they have failed to repent and are a godless and evil people. False prophets have led them astray. They consume each other, so God will pour out His wrath through Assyria.

Judgment on Arrogant Assyria (10:5–19)

The Lord will destroy Assyria for its arrogance. Like a saw or an axe, Assyria is simply the instrument God has chosen. After He accomplishes His purposes against Israel and Judah, He will judge Assyria.

SET THE SCENE

Assyria's War Crimes and Atrocities

Assyria brutally mistreated its enemies and reveled in torture. Archaeologists have found many ancient inscriptions, carvings, and annals celebrating this wanton violence.

Where else in the Bible do we see this transition between God's words of warning and promises of restoration?

The Remnant of Israel Will Return (10:20–34)

Though God's people will suffer many things, He will restore a remnant. This restoration to the land will take place in the distant future, when a remnant will return to Judah from Babylonian exile.

The Righteous Reign of the Branch (11:1–16)

When God returns His exiled people to their land, He will raise up a Branch from the family line of Jesse (King David's father). This righteous King will not only bring peace but also restore creation.

The LORD Is My Strength and My Song (12:1–6)

God's people will sing a new song when they return from exile. We will sing it in the new creation at Christ's second coming, and in the meantime, we praise God for His wonderful acts toward us in Christ.

Oracles About the Nations (13:1–23:18)

Isaiah continues with eleven oracles, or prophecies, against surrounding foreign nations. This section warns of the day of the Lord, which is ultimately Christ returning on the Last Day to judge the whole world.

The Judgment of Babylon (13:1–22)

VISUALIZE

WAYPOINT

What does this text show us?

Just as God had used Assyria to punish Israel's sins, He will use Babylon to punish wicked Assyria and Jerusalem. Isaiah further prophesies that Babylon will also be destroyed one day and laid desolate by the Medes (or Persians).

How could those who believed Isaiah's message find comfort in the promised destruction of Babylon?

Babylon came to represent all of Satan's evil rule in this world. How does Jesus' death and resurrection assure the downfall of Satan's kingdom?

Looking into your different vocations or places of responsibility in life, how can you share the hope of the Gospel to people in your life right now?

What does this text reveal about God's plan of salvation?
In the centuries to come, one empire will replace another. Yet God makes all these events advance His plan of salvation. During this rise and fall of empires, the Messiah will be born in Bethlehem and bring about God's kingdom.

What does this text uncover about our identity and calling as God's people today?
All who refuse to confess their sin and who die apart from faith in Christ will experience the eternal torment of hell. This message spurs us on to share the Gospel with everyone God has placed in our lives.

The Restoration of Jacob (14:1–2)

Despite the pain and destruction that the Babylonians will cause, God promises to bring His exiles back to their land and restore their fortunes, giving them a position of privilege above their enemies.

Israel's Remnant Taunts Babylon (14:3–23)

After Assyria and Babylon fall, all their arrogant boasts about their gods' power over the true God will be revealed as folly.

CLEAR THE CONFUSION

What are some things our society holds up as Day Stars for us—that is, things that promise to provide everything we will ever need?

Why did Isaiah refer to the king of Babylon as the Day Star (v. 12)?

The Day Star is the planet Venus, which is seen at early dawn at certain times of the year. Before reaching its summit, the sun rises and Venus's glory disappears. Likewise, the king of Babylon would never replace the true God.

An Oracle Concerning Assyria (14:24–27)

This oracle is against Assyria, whom God will bring low after using them to serve only His epic purposes.

An Oracle Concerning Philistia (14:28–32)

This prophecy confronts the Philistines for rejoicing at the apparent downfall of Judah under the onslaught of the Assyrians. God will defend Judah, but the Philistines will be destroyed by Assyria's advance.

An Oracle Concerning Moab (15:1–16:14)

The Moabites will suffer God's punishment within three years of this prophecy. Yet, in this oracle, God promises the Messiah, who will come one day for all who believe in God's promises (16:5).

An Oracle Concerning Damascus (17:1–14)

Because Syria has allied itself with the Northern Kingdom of Israel, Assyria will destroy Damascus and Samaria, the capitals of both nations. Yet a remnant of Gentile Syrians will remain to await the coming Messiah.

An Oracle Concerning Cush (18:1–7)

Cush, south of Egypt, will not need to fight the Assyrians because Israel's God will cut down the invaders Himself. One day, the people of Cush will bring tribute to Zion, showing God's promise is for all nations.

Why was Egypt a vain hope for Judah? What are some vain hopes people rely on today?

An Oracle Concerning Egypt (19:1–15)

Egypt attempts to stand up against the Assyrian invasion. Yet Egypt's hope is foolish because they trust in their false gods. Though they offer resistance against the Assyrians, they cannot stand against God.

Egypt, Assyria, Israel Blessed (19:16–25)

Isaiah prophesies a future age when God will discipline the Egyptians and they will worship Him alone. Even more, so will the Assyrians, and God's peace will be on all these currently warring nations.

A Sign Against Egypt and Cush (20:1–6)

Judah looks to Egypt and Cush for protection from Assyria. Isaiah prophesies that they will be captured and led into exile by the Assyrians. God's people must look to Him alone for rescue from their enemies.

CLEAR THE CONFUSION

Why did Isaiah walk naked and barefoot for three years?

This sign warned Judah that they would also be stripped naked, beaten, and led into captivity by the Assyrians if they did not trust God for rescue. Blessedly, King Hezekiah heeded Isaiah's message and God saved them from Assyria.

PICTURE OF THE SAVIOR

Nakedness: Isaiah and Jesus

The Gospels do not state that Jesus was naked on the cross, but that was common practice in Roman crucifixions. This is clearly implied in John 19:23–24, when the soldiers divided Jesus' garments and cast lots for His tunic.

Why would the exiles of Judah be happy when they heard the news "Fallen is Babylon!"? Think of a time God delivered you from great peril.

Fallen, Fallen Is Babylon (21:1–17)

The prophecies continue with oracles against Babylon, Dumah (Edom), and Arabia. The Babylonian prophecy speaks to the more distant future, while the prophecies against Edom and Arabia are more imminent.

An Oracle Concerning Jerusalem (22:1–25)

After many prophecies against foreign nations, God turns to His people in Jerusalem. God calls out their past and present sins, showing they, too, will suffer His judgment.

SET THE SCENE

Hezekiah's Tunnel

Isaiah mentions a water system Hezekiah built during the siege for Jerusalem. Archaeologists uncovered a system of springs and reservoirs into Jerusalem. This famous "Hezekiah's Tunnel" is a popular tourist destination to this day.

An Oracle Concerning Tyre and Sidon (23:1–18)

These northern neighbors of Israel had often been political allies of God's people, but they worshiped false gods and often led God's people astray. Their great trade wealth is compared to prostitution.

Cosmic Judgment (24:1–27:13)

This next section shows both God's ultimate judgment on the whole earth and the redemption of God's people in the person and work of Christ. This section offers us a unique and poignant view of our messianic hope!

Judgment on the Whole Earth (24:1–23)

The scene shifts to the final judgment. Isaiah makes it clear that no unbeliever will escape God's wrath. The sins of the world will be punished, and God will reveal His ultimate glory at the end of the age.

LINK BETWEEN THE TESTAMENTS

The End Times (Isaiah 24 → Matthew 25:31–46)

Isaiah and Jesus both talked of a final end-times judgment brought about by God's angel armies. All people deserve punishment for our sins. But Jesus bore our punishment on the cross, so God will not punish us as we deserve.

God Will Swallow Up Death Forever (25:1–12)

How did God swallow up death forever on Mount Calvary through Jesus' cross and empty tomb?

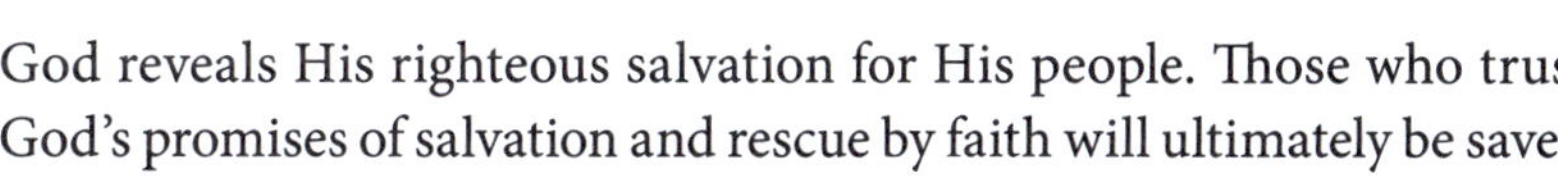

God reveals His righteous salvation for His people. Those who trust God's promises of salvation and rescue by faith will ultimately be saved from His wrath on the Last Day and freed from eternal death.

You Keep Him in Perfect Peace (26:1–21)

God removes His people's enemies and gives the world peace. God's people, claimed by Christ, will rise to new, eternal life in the new creation, and those who oppose God will be no more.

The Redemption of Israel (27:1–13)

VISUALIZE

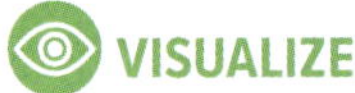

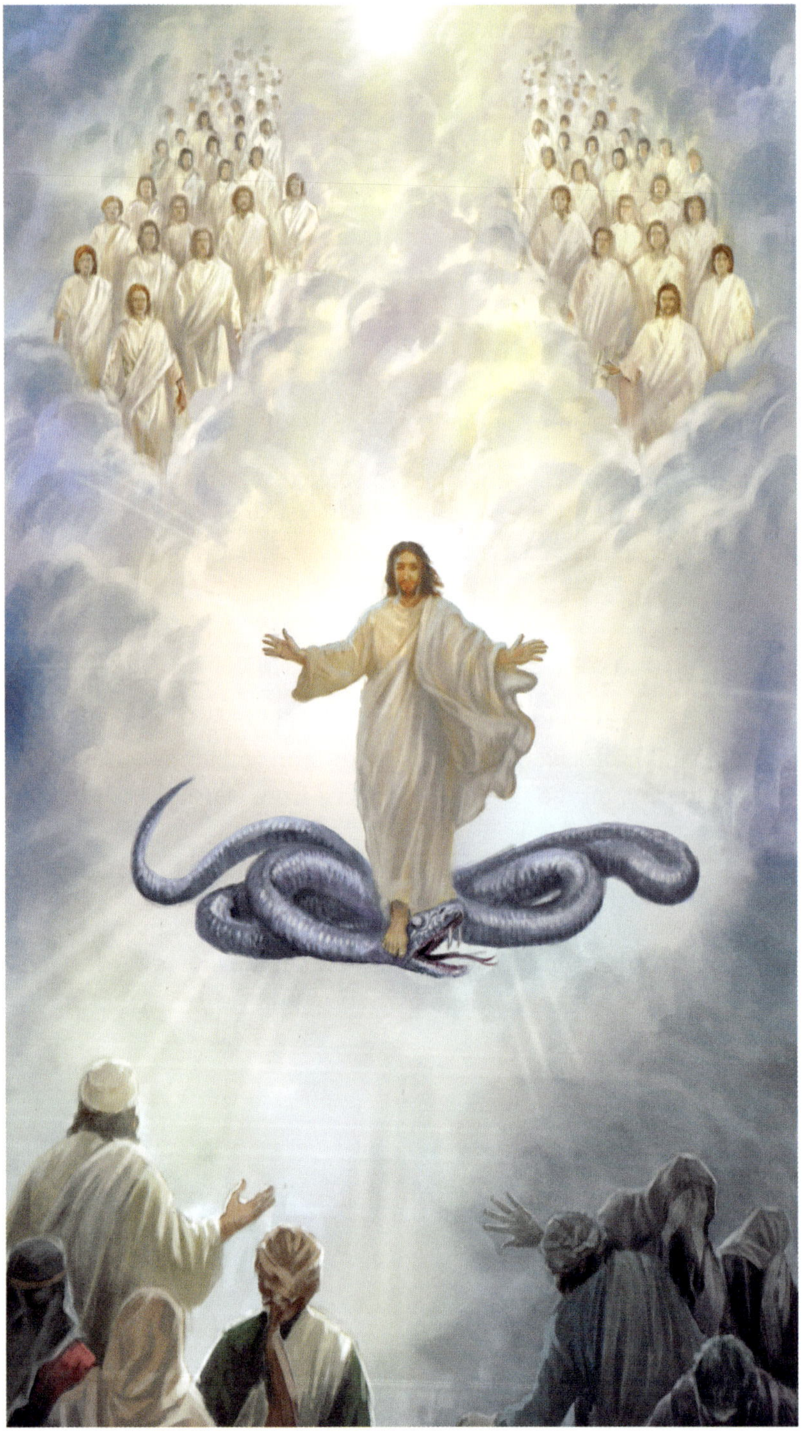

WAYPOINT

What does this text show us?
This section of end-times prophecy concludes with the slaying of Leviathan, the sea dragon, which clearly represents Satan. With the devil defeated and sin atoned for, God's people will only bear the good fruit of good works.

What does this text reveal about God's plan of salvation?
Like a loving vineyard owner caring for his vines, so God will care for us forever. This is the great gift of Jesus, who won the victory on the cross over sin, death, and the devil for all times for us.

What does this text uncover about our identity and calling as God's people today?
God's promise has been fulfilled for us in Christ. Though we may feel helpless and hopeless, we are not to give in. Instead, we look to the victory won for us in Christ and the promise of the new creation for God's people.

The Israelites feared the seas, especially the great creatures that lived there. What comfort would they draw from God's promise here?

Why was it essential that Jesus defeat the devil through His death and resurrection?

When you feel weak and overwhelmed, how can this passage give you strength and confidence?

Ephraim (Samaria) and Jerusalem (28:1–32:20)

In this section, God promises destruction and restoration—destruction because nations did not seek God or His protection; restoration resulting from the destruction of the Assyrians and the Messiah's coming.

Judgment on Ephraim and Jerusalem (28:1–13)

God once again points to the pride of the Northern Kingdom (Ephraim) and, by extension, Judah in the south. The Assyrians will show God's justice, but God will preserve a remnant following the conquest.

A Cornerstone in Zion (28:14–29)

The people of Jerusalem feel secure in their earthly covenants. But not even death can save them from God's judgment. All will be raised on the Last Day; only those who believe in God's promises are truly safe.

Consider criminals who think they can avoid facing justice by killing themselves, even when Isaiah tells us not even death can save us from God's judgment. How are they deluding themselves?

CLEAR THE CONFUSION

What was Israel's covenant with death (v. 15)?

This was not an actual covenant with death but one Jerusalem's leaders made with Egypt to protect them from the Assyrians. It was a covenant with death because Egypt could not stop Assyria, whom God had sent to discipline Israel.

The Siege of Jerusalem (29:1–24)

In Hebrew, *Ariel* means the "altar hearth of God" and refers to God's temple. Jerusalem will be besieged by the Assyrians, bringing God's people low. But God Himself will intervene and redeem His people.

LINK BETWEEN THE TESTAMENTS

The Deaf Shall Hear and the Eyes of the Blind Shall See (Isaiah 29:18–19 → Matthew 11:4–6)

Isaiah used these words to show how the proud would be humbled and the poor and humble would be exalted. Jesus used these words when John the Baptist was imprisoned and sent messengers to ask Jesus if He was the Christ.

SET THE SCENE

Ancient Siege Tactics

In a siege, an army surrounded a city, preventing escape or reinforcement. In the besieged city, supplies of food and water dwindled, causing starvation and disease. Sieges were only broken by supply shortages or enemy attack.

Name some sinful coping mechanisms people keep going back to when they find themselves under stress. How is that like Israel going back to Egypt?

Do Not Go Down to Egypt (30:1–7)

God's people look for protection and aid from Egypt. How ironic that the people God had delivered from Egypt during the exodus are willing to resubmit themselves to Egypt rather than trust in the Lord's protection.

A Rebellious People (30:8–17)

God accuses His people of rebellion, like foolish, lying children. They refuse to hear and believe God's Word, so they will be demolished. Yet God will grant quietness and strength to those who trust His promises.

The LORD Will Be Gracious (30:18–33)

God promises His people that there will be a time when He will defeat the Assyrians and restore Jerusalem. As in many prophecies, this vision also foreshadows the ultimate restoration in the new creation.

Woe to Those Who Go Down to Egypt (31:1–9)

God warns Judah not to trust in Egypt. Instead, God promises He will destroy the Assyrians and save His people in Jerusalem. These promises will give King Hezekiah and Jerusalem courage to trust God.

A King Will Reign in Righteousness (32:1–8)

Isaiah describes the rule of the future messianic King. The righteous King and those whom He has appointed to help rule (princes) will provide for His people while God exposes the fools and unwise.

PICTURE OF THE SAVIOR

The Coming King

God slowly put together a picture of the Messiah. The coming King rules in righteousness. Those who repent of their sin will receive forgiveness as He shares His righteousness. In Christ, God opens eyes and ears by His Word.

Complacent Women Warned of Disaster (32:9–20)

God warns the women in Jerusalem who believe nothing bad will come that disaster will befall their country under the Assyrians. He then promises an age when the Spirit will be poured out on His people.

The Hinge of the Book (33:1–35:10)

The first half of Isaiah focuses mainly on the problems Jerusalem had brought on itself by its sins and relationships to foreign powers. The rest of the book focuses on Jerusalem in other ways and with a different tone.

How much can earthly rulers influence our lives for good or for ill?

O LORD, Be Gracious to Us (33:1–24)

Isaiah cries to God for grace and receives it. He looks forward to a King who will rule in righteousness and peace. Though in some ways this points to King Hezekiah, this is a messianic prophecy of Jesus Christ.

Judgment on the Nations (34:1–17)

Isaiah's prophecy returns to familiar themes of God's wrath against the nations, which will be laid desolate. Yet praise be to God that He promises forgiveness for all who believe His promises.

LINK BETWEEN THE TESTAMENTS

Judged by a Just God (Isaiah 34 → Romans 2)

God's wrath and mercy are evident in both the Old and New Testaments. Romans 2 bears a striking similarity to Isaiah 34. A holy God cannot let evil go unpunished. However, in His mercy, God punished Jesus in our place.

The Ransomed Shall Return (35:1–10)

Why would it be important for the Judean exiles to have this promise during their seventy years of exile in Babylon?

In what ways did Jesus' healing miracles begin restoring Adam and Eve's children from their fall into sin?

When we help our neighbor in times of need, how does that open an opportunity to share Christ's great restoration?

WAYPOINT

What does this text show us?
In one way, this prophecy speaks of the return from exile after captivity in Babylon. In a much greater way, it points to the final restoration of all things when Christ returns in glory.

What does this text reveal about God's plan of salvation?
During His earthly ministry, Jesus refers to Himself as the one who does miracles and brings about restoration. His miracles not only point to what God will do at the end of all things but even begin that restoration here and now.

What does this text uncover about our identity and calling as God's people today?
Jesus came to bring eternal life and salvation through the cross and the empty tomb, but He also cared for the needs of those around Him. As we follow Christ, we love and serve our neighbor while sharing the Gospel with them.

Isaiah and Hezekiah (36:1–39:8)

The events in this section form the central event of Isaiah: the destruction of the Assyrian army at God's hand. These events are also told in 2 Kings 18–20 and 2 Chronicles 32.

Sennacherib Invades Judah (36:1–22)

After successfully conquering Judah's other fortified cities, the Assyrians' military leader is sent to Jerusalem. Within earshot of the people, he warns that the Assyrians will show no mercy unless Jerusalem surrenders.

Hezekiah Seeks Isaiah's Help (37:1–13)

Hezekiah tears his clothes and sends a messenger to Isaiah. Through Isaiah, God assures Hezekiah the Assyrians will return home. Though Sennacherib departs to face advances by Cush, he promises to return.

Hezekiah's Prayer for Deliverance (37:14–20)

Hezekiah takes Sennacherib's letter and goes to the temple to pray. As God's anointed king, he offers up a humble prayer for deliverance for Judah. He recalls God's promises to His people.

Sennacherib's Fall (37:21–38)

How is this salvation from the Lord similar to the tenth plague, the death of the firstborn in Egypt (Exodus 12:29–32)?

The Angel of the Lord delivered God's people completely by Himself. Why was it essential that Jesus defeated sin, death, and Satan all alone?

How does remembering Jesus' salvation from sin, death, and hell give you greater courage to pray for important things in this life?

Hezekiah might have thought it was wise to impress the Babylonian envoys with how much a small country like Judah had to offer Babylon. How could that thinking backfire in the future when Babylon conquered Assyria?

WAYPOINT

What does this text show us?
The Angel of the Lord slays 185,000 Assyrian soldiers during the night. The remnants of the Assyrian force return to Nineveh. There, the king is struck down by his sons while engaged in idol worship and God's prophecy is complete.

What does this text reveal about God's plan of salvation?
The Angel of the Lord, commonly interpreted as the preincarnate Christ, intervenes to destroy the Assyrians and preserve God's promises. This foreshadows Christ's intervention through His incarnation, death, and resurrection.

What does this text uncover about our identity and calling as God's people today?
God commands and invites us to pray, especially in times of trouble. We do so recalling that Jesus Christ has already overcome our existential threat: sin, death, and hell. We can and do pray, rejoicing in God's great victories for us.

Hezekiah's Sickness and Recovery (38:1–22)

Hezekiah becomes deathly ill. Isaiah tells him to prepare for death. Hezekiah prays for deliverance and God promises healing. Even more, God miraculously turns back the sun's shadow to reassure the king.

Envoys from Babylon (39:1–8)

Seeking allies against Assyria, Babylon sends an envoy to Hezekiah. God condemns Hezekiah's proud display of his wealth and seeking foreign powers for deliverance. God prophesies that Babylon will conquer Judah.

Comfort for the Lord's Weary People (40:1–31)

Chapter 40 stands out as a division unto itself. It has three herald declarations. The first is from God Himself, the second from the special messenger John the Baptist, and the third from the city of Jerusalem.

Comfort for God's People (40:1–5)

God promises to comfort and restore His people from exile in Babylon. Though undeserving, they receive a double portion of His mercy and grace. In verses 1–2, the first herald introduces the second herald, Christ's messenger, John the Baptist, who speaks in verses 3–8.

The Word of God Stands Forever (40:6–8)

The prophetic voice of the second herald, John the Baptist, continues proclaiming that, like grass, all things fade away. Only the Word of God stands forever, and what He promises will come to pass.

The Greatness of God (40:9–31)

The third herald, the city of Jerusalem itself, speaks of God's goodness to the surrounding nations. All foreign powers and false gods will fail, but the Lord God Himself will preserve and shepherd His people.

The Lord Chooses Israel, His Servant (41:1–42:17)

In this next section, God tells the Israelites of His unmerited mercy to them. He also foretells the coming of Christ, the great Servant, who stands in for Israel and fulfills their purpose in the world.

Fear Not, for I Am with You (41:1–20)

God assures Israel that He will bring down the surrounding nations and raise up His people. Christ has total authority over the earth and redeems God's people.

The Futility of Idols (41:21–29)

God challenges the unbelieving nations and their idols. Because of this idolatry, God prophesies the coming of Cyrus, king of Persia, who will overthrow the Babylonians and return Israel from exile.

The LORD's Chosen Servant (42:1–9)

What does this text show us?
The Servant is the promised Messiah. He will be set apart for God's purpose and filled with the Spirit, a gentle, just, and righteous miracle-worker and savior. The old covenant will pass away and a new one will take its place.

What does this text reveal about God's plan of salvation?
This is yet another "sighting" of the Messiah foretold in the Old Testament, revealing His bold yet gentle nature and His mission to give sight to the blind, be the light of the world, and rescue God's people from their enemies.

List all the references you see to Christ in this passage.

In what ways does this passage point both to God's past faithfulness in the Old Testament and to His upcoming faithfulness in the New Testament?

How are you tempted to fall into this sin of idolatry? How do these prophecies restore your focus on Jesus Christ, your Savior and Lord?

What does this text uncover about our identity and calling as God's people today?
We find our identity in the person and work of Christ. He has redeemed us from the powers of death and will bring us to the new creation, where all things will be made new and all sad things come untrue.

LINK BETWEEN THE TESTAMENTS

A Covenant for the People, a Light for the Nations (Isaiah 42:6 → Luke 2:32)

Isaiah promised the Messiah would make a new covenant between God and Israel through His suffering and death. He would be a light to the Gentile nations as they learned of His forgiveness through faith. When Joseph and Mary presented Jesus at the temple, Simeon took Jesus in his arms and, applying Isaiah's words, proclaimed that the child would be "a light for revelation to the Gentiles, and for glory to Your people Israel."

Sing to the LORD a New Song (42:10–17)

The Lord's Servant, the Messiah, casts down idols, turns darkness into light, and leads God's people in the way of truth. In response, the nations Christ has redeemed praise God and tell the good news of His salvation.

The Redemption of Israel (42:18–44:20)

The Servant in the previous chapters points to Christ, but the servant in this section refers to Israel, the disobedient nation. This servant will not follow God. Christ calls Israel to repentance, faith, and restoration.

Israel's Failure to Hear and See (42:18–25)

Israel will be exiled for its failure to live faithfully as God's chosen instrument in the world. This is the just punishment for their sins and sets up the good news God will declare to Israel in the upcoming chapters.

CLEAR THE CONFUSION

Why did God call His servant, the nation of Israel, blind and deaf (6:10)?

This recalls God's words when He commissioned Isaiah. Israel could read and hear God's Word, but they didn't understand the Law and Gospel or repent and believe in God's forgiveness for the sake of the coming Messiah.

Think of a time when it felt as though your life was shattered and you would never be happy again. How did the Lord bring you through that time?

Israel's Only Savior (43:1–28)

God repeatedly tells Israel to fear not! He will be with them as they go into exile and will bring them back again. After the return, He will give them a new and supernatural abundance, the forgiveness of sins.

Israel the LORD's Chosen (44:1–5)

God will not only bring Israel back; He will increase their people and their land by the Spirit. Today we can clearly see that God accomplishes this work through pouring out His Spirit in Word and Sacrament.

Besides Me There Is No God (44:6–8)

In the face of other nations with their idols, God reminds Israel that He alone is God. He is the one who rescues, or redeems, them. They have no need to give in to or fear earthly powers—He is their rock.

The Folly of Idolatry (44:9–20)

God uses a powerful illustration to show how foolish idolatry is. Humans make something and then worship it as though it were a god. They betray their own reason and senses to follow Satan's senseless lies.

VISUALIZE

Freedom from Babylon (44:21–48:22)

This next section focuses on Judah returning from exile (looking 150–200 years in the future). Isaiah's prophecies of future restoration serve as hopeful reminders of God's faithfulness during future generations of trial.

The LORD Redeems Israel (44:21–28)

God once again calls on Israel to remember His faithfulness. As He has guided and guarded them through all their days, He will deliver them from bondage through His chosen instrument, a ruler named Cyrus.

What comfort does it bring to know God controls even people who do not acknowledge Him?

Cyrus, God's Instrument (45:1–13)

God addresses the future king of Persia, Cyrus, as His instrument. Though Cyrus will not know the Lord, he will free God's people from exile. The Lord is God of all He created, and nothing is outside His control.

The LORD, the Only Savior (45:14–25)

WAYPOINT

What does this text show us?
The Lord has a special place and role for Israel. Yet He calls on all the nations to turn to Him and receive salvation (v. 22). He concludes by declaring the truth that righteousness and strength are found only in Him (v. 24).

What does this text reveal about God's plan of salvation?
God desires all people to hear His Word, turn in repentance, and receive salvation. His plan has always been to redeem the world, which by grace through faith in Christ receives the gifts of forgiveness, life, and salvation.

What does this text uncover about our identity and calling as God's people today?
Through His people, the church, God proclaims the Law and Gospel to the world. We support and continue that same mission to the nations today. We also have an opportunity to love and serve our neighbor in the name of Christ.

How did Israel fail in its mission to share God's holy name with the nations around it?

Why do you think Jesus' ministry was primarily to the lost people of Israel rather than to the nations around Israel?

How do we fail to honor God's name with the neighbors God has placed around us? With God's help, how can we live as light and salt to the world?

The Idols of Babylon and the One True God (46:1–13)

Babylon will be conquered by Cyrus, the Persian king. Though God's people must suffer defeat and exile in Babylon, they are to look to Him for righteousness and salvation.

The Humiliation of Babylon (47:1–15)

Babylon will be cast aside and all its power will be exposed as false, especially its astrology and sorcery. The God of Israel is the only true God. All other gods are false idols or demons in disguise.

Israel Refined for God's Glory (48:1–11)

God chastises Israel for its stubborn lack of repentance, which will drive Him to discipline them through exile. But through this, He will ensure that the promised Messiah will come into the world to redeem it.

The LORD's Call to Israel (48:12–22)

God declares His future victory over Babylon but laments the pain and destruction Israel could have avoided if they had only faithfully followed Him. This shows God's heart of love for His chosen people.

What bad things did your parents warn you to avoid? What hardships did you suffer because you ignored their teaching? How is God's Law like our parents' teachings?

The Suffering Servant and Redeemed Israel (49:1–55:13)

Isaiah now turns from future prophecies about Persia and Babylon to the Messiah. These seven chapters provide some of the most powerful and memorable prophecies about Jesus in all of the Old Testament.

The Servant of the LORD (49:1–7)

God speaks about being called to serve and redeem Israel. This clearly refers to the Messiah, the Christ. The Second Person of the Trinity will fulfill God's plan of salvation, even from the womb of the virgin.

LINK BETWEEN THE TESTAMENTS

Called from the Womb (Isaiah 49:1 → Luke 1:31–33)

Just as prophesied in Isaiah, the angel Gabriel visited the virgin Mary and announced that she would conceive and bear God's Son and name Him Jesus.

The Restoration of Israel (49:8–26)

After the pain of exile, God will bring the Israelites back to their land. Through this act of redemption, God will show the world His loving and faithful character.

Israel's Sin and the Servant's Obedience (50:1–11)

Isaiah returns to the theme of the obedient Servant in chapter 50. In verses 1–3, Israel serves as a foil for the Servant, who in verses 4–11 is faithful, humble, and walks in God's ways. This Servant is Christ.

PICTURE OF THE SAVIOR

Jesus' Suffering

Though Israel closed its eyes and ears to God's call, Jesus obeyed. During His trials, the Roman soldiers struck Jesus' back as they scourged Him and members of the Jewish high court slapped Jesus, spit upon Him, and struck Him.

Name something difficult God's Word directs you to do. Why is it difficult? How can Jesus' obedience to death on the cross inspire you to obey as well?

The LORD's Comfort for Zion (51:1–23)

God reminds His people of His faithfulness to them by, among other things, delivering them from Egypt. When they cry to Him for rescue, He asks why they fear mortal men rather than fearing Him.

The LORD's Coming Salvation (52:1–12)

God promises to return His people from exile. As He had delivered them from Egypt and conquered the Assyrians, He will also bring them back from Babylon. God's people cling to this prophetic hope for generations.

He Was Pierced for Our Transgressions (52:13–53:12)

What particular sections of this prophecy can you connect to the specific actions and events surrounding the death of Christ?

Compare the two servants, Israel and the Messiah. How is the Servant Messiah different from the servant Israel?

What is one way you can remind yourself today of Christ's great love for you?

Isaiah 54 speaks of God's anger overflowing for a moment but His steadfast love enduring forever. How can remembering this promise help when you are going through times of struggle?

WAYPOINT

What does this text show us?

God foretells that Christ would willingly take the sins of the world upon Himself to make many righteous before God and make intercession for the transgressors.

What does this text reveal about God's plan of salvation?

This song uncovers for God's people the heart of Christ: desiring to bring reconciliation and peace between sinful humanity and a righteous God. All this suffering and pain would bring with it the reconciliation of the world.

What does this text uncover about our identity and calling as God's people today?

Out of a desire to make you righteous before God, Christ laid aside His glory, was despised by His own creatures, and suffered the agony of death. Remember His love for you today and every day, and live your Christian freedom with joy.

The Eternal Covenant of Peace (54:1–17)

God declares His covenant of peace. His people will not need to fear or be ashamed. This vision of the future, when nobody will be able to harm God's people, will come to pass at Christ's second coming.

The Compassion of the LORD (55:1–13)

Listening to God's Word is like eating a meal that satisfies. The descendant of David—that is, Jesus—will bear witness to God's Word, bringing the world life and salvation.

Understanding Divine Character (56:1–66:24)

God does not desire for any to perish eternally but that all would come to saving faith. Through that faith, God provides a new, restored life in the new heaven and the new earth. This is ours through Christ.

Salvation for Foreigners (56:1–8)

God's salvation is not only for the Israelites but for all who believe His promises. This expands the scope of God's saving mission to all of Adam and Eve's children. Saving faith determines one's standing before God.

Why is it easy to underestimate the threat that the devil, the world, and our sinful nature are to our eternal salvation?

Israel's Irresponsible Leaders (56:9–12)

Israel's leaders have failed to spiritually guide and guard God's people. They think the day of judgment will never come. We, too, should be on guard against the devil, the world, and our sinful flesh.

Israel's Futile Idolatry (57:1–13)

God tracks the idolatry of His people throughout their history, from petty selfishness, to pagan sensuality, to child sacrifice. Despite this harsh language, however, those who take refuge in Him will inherit the land.

SET THE SCENE

The Ancient Fascination with Sorcery and the Occult

Satanic arts use spells and incantations to coerce God to do what the practitioner wants or to take dominion from Him. Since such practices lead people from God and toward Satan's influence, God strictly forbids them throughout the Bible.

Comfort for the Contrite (57:14–21)

God exhorts His people to prepare for His coming. Though He warns against unrepentance and sliding back into sin, God will restore His people and give comfort to the repentant.

True and False Fasting (58:1–14)

In Isaiah's time, the people used fasting as a substitute for doing good works. God commands us to earnestly and honestly do good works in response to His love. God again reveals His heart of love for His creatures.

Evil and Oppression (59:1–15a)

This passage is a confession of our sins and the way those sins damage the fabric of society. Near the end of the book of Isaiah, we pan out and see the epic picture of God's ways among all fallen human creatures.

Judgment and Redemption (59:15b–21)

God again reveals His epic plan of salvation. Seeing that humanity is fallen and there is no way man can redeem himself, God will send a Redeemer. He will arise from Israel but will redeem the world.

What consequences of sin (your own sin, the sins of others, or living under the curse) do you most look forward to Jesus removing?

The Future Glory of Israel (60:1–22)

God reveals the restoration of creation at Christ's second coming. All the pain and suffering of God's people as a consequence of their own sin will be removed when the Redeemer makes all things new.

The Year of the LORD's Favor (61:1–11)

The Messiah will bring good news to the poor and brokenhearted. God uses Law to humble the proud, who do not think they need God, and the Gospel to raise up those crushed by the Law.

LINK BETWEEN THE TESTAMENTS

The Year of the Lord's Favor (Isaiah 61:1–2 → Luke 4:18–19)

When Jesus preached in the synagogue in His hometown of Nazareth, He unrolled the scroll of Isaiah, found this very passage, and began His sermon with these verses from Isaiah.

Zion's Coming Salvation (62:1–12)

God speaks about what He will do for Jerusalem in the age of the Messiah. Jerusalem will be saved and its people called The Holy People. When Christ returns, He will gather God's people from every location.

The idea of God punishing unbelievers eternally in hell is unnerving. Why is it important to honestly wrestle with God's holiness and perfect justice?

The LORD's Day of Vengeance (63:1–6)

When Christ returns at the end of the world, He will finally remove His enemies and enact justice for His people. Only when these sources of evil are removed can Christ restore His creation to utter perfection.

The LORD's Mercy Remembered (63:7–14)

As recounted in the exodus narrative, God had shown who He is and what He does for His people. The cross and empty tomb will complete that narrative as God in Christ delivers His people from eternal death.

Prayer for Mercy (63:15–64:12)

This passage serves as a model prayer for God's people. It beautifully directs us not only to praise Him for His goodness but also to offer up prayers of request and intercession during uncertain times.

LINK BETWEEN THE TESTAMENTS

Treasures in Jars of Clay (Isaiah 64:8 → 2 Corinthians 4:7)

Isaiah reminds us that God is our potter and we are the clay. He is the Creator; we are the creation. Paul adds that we are fragile vessels filled to the brim with the blessings of God's grace and mercy. Though we are weak, He is strong.

Judgment and Salvation (65:1–16)

God contrasts those who reject Him with those who trust in Him. Judgment will come upon all who reject God, while safety and security will come for those who have faith in His promises.

New Heavens and a New Earth (65:17–25)

WAYPOINT

What does this text show us?
God will create new heavens and a new earth, and the former things will not be remembered by those who dwell there. Death itself (along with mourning and weeping) will be abolished in this new creation, and we will live forever.

What does this text reveal about God's plan of salvation?
Isaiah depicts the future end to the story of salvation: Jesus' return. We look to the day when Jesus comes to make all things new and we boldly take our place among the saints in the new life to come.

What does this text uncover about our identity and calling as God's people today?
Like the saints in the Bible, we have a place in God's epic plan of salvation. He made us His own through the Gospel and calls us to love and serve our neighbor in our various stations in life.

What are some specifics Isaiah mentions that distinguish the new heavens and the new earth from the present heaven and earth?

Why do you think God chose to redeem His fallen creation rather than destroy it and start again?

How can it transform our daily lives to think of the "resurrection of the dead and the life of the world to come" (Nicene Creed)?

The Humble and Contrite in Spirit (66:1–6)

God rejoices in the humble of heart but brings down those who delight in abominations. We humbly confess our sins to God, receive His mercy, and go back into the world living by His ways and not our own.

Rejoice with Jerusalem (66:7–14)

God relates His glory returning to His people to a mother giving birth to a son before ever going into labor. On Judgment Day, when Christ returns, we will be raised and changed instantly to live in glory forever.

Final Judgment and Glory of the LORD (66:15–24)

The prophecy of Isaiah comes to a conclusion. All will see God's glory. Those who believe will experience God's glory with joy. Unbelievers will experience God's glory in terror and destruction.

LINK BETWEEN THE TESTAMENTS

The Fires of Hell → The Rich Man and Lazarus (Isaiah 66:24 → Luke 16:19–31)

Is hell anything more than physical death? Isaiah taught that the worm that devours the dead body will never die, while the fire that burns it will never be quenched, meaning hell lasts forever. In Luke 16, Jesus taught that unbelievers will suffer torment in the flames after death (consider Mark 9:43–48 as well). Both passages teach us not to underestimate the wrath of God, which Jesus willingly suffered in our place.

JEREMIAH

Welcome to Jeremiah

In the very first chapter of Jeremiah, God calls Jeremiah His "iron" prophet (v. 18). Jeremiah needs every bit of the iron strength God will provide as the Lord directs him to deliver difficult messages regarding God's impending judgment. Yet, despite this difficult news, he also clearly prophesies the coming of the promised Savior, Jesus Christ. As you read Jeremiah, think of your guilt and sin, which Jesus took upon Himself, suffering God's terrible wrath so that you may live in peace eternally.

What do you already know about the prophet Jeremiah?

Jeremiah at a Glance

- **Start:** The book of Jeremiah begins with God's call to Jeremiah to serve as His prophet.
- **End:** The book of Jeremiah concludes by pronouncing God's judgment against the nations for their unfaithfulness.
- **Theme:** Jeremiah calls Judah to repentance and prophesies both the coming Babylonian exile and the promised Messiah.
- **Author and Date:** The book of Jeremiah was written by the prophet Jeremiah along with his scribe Baruch. The text was completed sometime between 628 and 580 BC.
- **Places Visited:** Anathoth (in the tribe of Benjamin), Judah, and Jerusalem; events also in Egypt, Babylon, Assyria, and other places
- **Journey Time:** The fifty-two chapters of Jeremiah can be read in approximately four hours.
- **Outline:**
    - The Call of Jeremiah (1:1–19)
    - Prophecy Against Judah (2:1–35:19)
    - Jeremiah's Suffering and Persecution (36:1–38:28)
    - The Fall of Jerusalem (39:1–45:5)
    - Judgment Against the Nations (46:1–51:64)
    - Historical Appendix (52:1–34)

Five Top Sights and Spectacles of Jeremiah

Jeremiah's Grief (8:18–9:26) Stand alongside Jeremiah as he experiences intense grief over the people.

Drought and Famine (14:1–12) Experience the gnawing thirst and hunger as Judah suffers drought and famine.

Jeremiah Punished by Pashhur (20:1–18) Share in Jeremiah's pain as he is unfairly punished by the priest Pashhur for faithfully speaking God's message.

Promises for God's People (32:36–33:26) Sense the hope as God promises to remain with and restore His faithful followers.

Jerusalem Falls (39:1–10) Witness the destruction of Jerusalem as the Babylonian army defeats Judah.

Seeing Jesus in Jeremiah

Chapters 30–33 of Jeremiah give us some of the clearest prophecies about the promised Messiah, Jesus Christ. Jeremiah was so associated with the coming Savior that when Jesus questions His disciples concerning who the people say He is, Peter confesses, "Some say John the Baptist, others say Elijah, and others Jeremiah or one of the prophets" (Matthew 16:14).

The Call of Jeremiah (1:1–19)

God raises up Jeremiah, a priest, to be His prophet to the people of Jerusalem and Judah.

Introduction (1:1–3)

Jeremiah's father was Hilkiah, a descendant of Abiathar, the high priest banished by King Solomon (1 Kings 2:26–27). Jeremiah served during the reigns of the last five kings of Judah.

The Call of Jeremiah (1:4–19)

WAYPOINT

What does this text show us?
God appointed Jeremiah to be a prophet before his birth. God reassures young Jeremiah He will give him the words to speak. The Lord promises to make him an iron pillar—a strong defender for the Lord.

What does this text reveal about God's plan of salvation?
Judah's idolatry, violence, and oppression threaten God's plan to send the Messiah through them as He promised. God raises up Jeremiah to drive the people from their sin and false worship toward the true God.

What does this text uncover about our identity and calling as God's people today?
Just as God called Jeremiah, in Baptism He calls every one of us as His own children. Through His Word, He guides us to serve Him in all that we do.

What questions do you have about God's message to Jeremiah?

God's message of destruction sounds quite alarming. How can we read this message and yet feel assured of God's mercy?

?

What has God called you to do in your everyday life to share His Word with others?

Prophecy Against Judah (2:1–35:19)

Jeremiah condemns the sins and idolatry of Jerusalem and the kingdom of Judah, warning of coming destruction if they do not repent.

Israel Forsakes the LORD (2:1–3:5)

When God led Israel out of Egypt and through the wilderness, they were devoted to the Lord as a young bride. But now they have broken their marriage vows, turning away from God to follow their own path.

Judah follows their sinful sister, Israel, into false worship and will suffer the consequences for their sin. How do you face this same issue in your life?

Faithless Israel Called to Repentance (3:6–4:4)

God warns Judah against following their faithless sister, Israel, into temptation. During the days of faithful King Josiah, the people outwardly celebrated the Passover, but their hearts were still chasing after false gods.

Disaster from the North (4:5–18)

Jeremiah warns of destruction coming from the north. The people of Jerusalem and other fortified cities will take refuge behind their walls. But the armies of Babylon will bring destruction to all of Judah.

CLEAR THE CONFUSION

Why did Jeremiah claim that God had utterly deceived His people (v. 10)?

The people believed the false prophets who promised that God would protect Judah from Babylon. Jeremiah is expressing his horror at the suffering Judah is bringing upon themselves because of their stubborn refusal to repent.

Jeremiah is called the weeping prophet because of the deep sorrow he felt when God punished His people. How can we learn from Jeremiah to be more concerned about unbelievers who are stirring God's wrath through their unrepentance?

Anguish over Judah's Desolation (4:19–31)

Jeremiah laments the coming destruction of Judah. They do not seek God but, like Jezebel in 2 Kings 9:30, adorn themselves in vain for lovers who despise them. Yet the Lord promises He will not utterly destroy Judah.

VISUALIZE

Destruction from the North

Babylon lay north of Judah and the city of Jerusalem. This map explains Jeremiah's prophecy concerning the destruction of Judah. As you work through the book of Jeremiah, refer back to this map to follow Jeremiah's warnings.

Jerusalem Refused to Repent (5:1–13)

From the king to the average man on the street, God calls all of Jerusalem to repent. But they rebel and worship false gods. God longs to forgive and restore His people, but they ignore His calling.

The LORD Proclaims Judgment (5:14–31)

Even though God's created world obeys the limits He set for it, sinful humans defy Him at every turn. As punishment for their unfaithfulness, God will allow a powerful foreign nation to destroy their kingdom.

What does God's rejection of Judah's offerings given without true repentance tell us about our repentance and forgiveness?

Impending Disaster for Jerusalem (6:1–30)

God will send northern armies to destroy Jerusalem. He has rejected their sacrifices because they are given without true repentance. The armies of the north are gathering to begin their advance on Jerusalem.

CLEAR THE CONFUSION

What did God use the image of metals and fire to illustrate (vv. 27–30)?

A refiner melts precious metals (like silver) in order to separate out the impure materials (like lead, bronze, and iron), which float to the surface and can be removed. But Judah refused to let go of their sin, repent, and be purified.

Evil in the Land (7:1–29)

The Lord tells Jeremiah to stand at the gate of the temple and warn the worshipers against thinking they can sin with impunity as long as they go to the temple afterward.

CLEAR THE CONFUSION

Who was the "queen of heaven" (v. 18)?

This refers to an astral deity, the planet Venus, which the Babylonians worshiped as a goddess, or possibly Ishtar, the goddess of war and sexual love or fertility. The unfaithful people of Judah worshiped this false goddess.

LINK BETWEEN THE TESTAMENTS

The Temple as a Den of Robbers → Jesus Cleanses the Temple (Jeremiah 7:10–11 → Matthew 21:12–13; Mark 11:15–17; Luke 19:45–46)

Because of false worship, God called the Jerusalem temple a den of robbers. When Jesus found the temple courts being used as a marketplace for the sale of sacrificial animals, He made a whip to drive out the people and animals, saying they had turned His Father's house of prayer into a den of robbers.

The Valley of Slaughter (7:30–8:3)

God condemns the people's willing sacrifice of their own children to false gods. The place where they gather will soon be called the "Valley of Slaughter." Their bodies will be desecrated and left to rot.

Sin and Treachery (8:4–17)

Despite God's warnings through Jeremiah, the religious leaders lead the people astray, claiming peace when there is none. The Lord compares the coming destruction to untamed serpents sent to bite the people.

Jeremiah grieves over the sins of his people. How do we cause God grief?

Jeremiah Grieves for His People (8:18–9:26)

The people of Judah speak peaceful words to one another but secretly plan to ambush each other. The Lord renews His warning to those who do not repent or trust in the Lord's covenant.

VISUALIZE

CLEAR THE CONFUSION

What does the phrase "balm in Gilead" mean (8:22)?

Gilead was the Israelite territory east of the Jordan River. It produced a spice made from tree gum that ancient people valued for its healing properties. But since Judah's sin was spiritual, no balm or earthly physician could heal it.

Idols and the Living God (10:1–25)

People cut down a tree, a craftsman decorates it with precious metals and fabric, but the resulting idol is as immobile as a scarecrow. No idol is like the true God. At His voice, the world is created and sustained.

The Broken Covenant (11:1–23)

The people of Judah willingly break the covenant the Lord made with Israel when He brought them out of Egypt. The people of Anathoth, Jeremiah's hometown, plot to kill him rather than obey God's message.

CLEAR THE CONFUSION

Why did God tell Jeremiah not to pray for the people (v. 14)?

God had sent His prophets urging the people to repent and turn from their sinfulness, yet the people continued to ignore His direction and mistreat His prophets. The time for interceding on behalf of the people had expired.

Jeremiah's Complaint (12:1–4)

Jeremiah is struggling with God's delay in punishing his enemies in Anathoth because they continue to thrive. Jeremiah asks how long God will permit them to continue with their evil.

Jeremiah's faith needed to grow more firm to face the rising persecution to come. How strong do you consider your faith to be? How can you seek God's help to make it stronger still?

The LORD Answers Jeremiah (12:5–17)

God allows time for people to repent. After He has plucked them out of the land and sent them into exile, He will restore them and even plant believing Gentiles among them in Christ's kingdom.

CLEAR THE CONFUSION

What is the thicket of the Jordan (v. 5)?

The banks of the Jordan River were a dense thicket, a perfect hiding place for Asiatic lions. It was a powerful image of the intense persecution Jeremiah would face when Jerusalem was actually under siege.

The Ruined Loincloth (13:1–11)

Jeremiah wears a new loincloth, then hides it in a cleft of the rock, leaving it useless. Judah should cling to God like a new loincloth and glorify Him by living holy lives. But it is worthless like Jeremiah's loincloth.

VISUALIZE

Wearing a Loincloth

A loincloth was the early equivalent of underwear. In biblical times, men wore loincloths of soft leather; later, linen loincloths replaced the leather. The loincloth was worn against the skin and wrapped tightly around the waist underneath a robe and tunic.

The Jars Filled with Wine (13:12–14)

Jeremiah tells the people of Judah that God will fill them with drunkenness—that is, the cup of His wrath—which will stupefy and leave them powerless against destruction.

CLEAR THE CONFUSION

Why did God use drunkenness as an image of His wrath?

Victims of war resemble people in a drunken stupor, stumbling around in a daze, not recognizing friend from foe, helpless to defend themselves. Those who refuse to repent will have to drink from His cup of wrath on Judgment Day.

Exile Threatened (13:15–27)

Those of both high office and low will be taken into exile, scattered like chaff blown in the wind. Enemies from the north will bring shame upon Judah for their arrogance and idolatry.

SET THE SCENE

What is exile?

When people are exiled, they are removed from their homeland by force. An enemy nation removes the conquered people in order to occupy the land they have defeated, or simply as punishment against the defeated nation.

Pestilence is defined as a plague or disease. While the text doesn't explain exactly the type of pestilence the people suffered, we can certainly understand the suffering it may have caused. What might be a modern-day equivalent to pestilence?

Famine, Sword, and Pestilence (14:1–12)

The Lord tells Jeremiah of a drought that will affect every aspect of life. Though the people cry to God for help (vv. 7–9) and appear to be sincere, God knows they are just looking for relief and are not truly repentant.

Lying Prophets (14:13–22)

False prophets directly contradict Jeremiah, promising peace and security. God tells Jeremiah these false teachers will be consumed by His punishment when Jeremiah's words stand and theirs fall.

The LORD Will Not Relent (15:1–9)

Even if Moses and Samuel interceded for this people, God would still punish the Israelites. The destroyers will carry out God's judgment against Jerusalem, yet the people will not repent and turn from their sins.

Jeremiah's Complaint (15:10–21)

Jeremiah seeks God's help to handle the pushback and persecution of his enemies. The Lord tells Jeremiah that his honest repentance will indeed rescue him from suffering the fate that awaits the people of Judah.

CLEAR THE CONFUSION

What did God mean when He told Jeremiah, "If you return, I will restore you" (v. 19)?

In verse 18, Jeremiah came very close to blaspheming God. Jeremiah needed to repent and return to the Lord. Then God would restore and strengthen him against the persecution he suffered. God promised to save and deliver him.

Famine, Sword, and Death (16:1–13)

Jeremiah must not marry or have children because whole families will die. He must not enter a house for a feast or when death strikes because there will be no celebrating or grieving when Jerusalem is besieged.

The LORD Will Restore Israel (16:14–21)

Judah will suffer doubly for their sin and idolatry, first in their homeland and again as they are taken away into exile. But all nations will witness the Lord's restoration when He returns them to the Promised Land.

An iron pen and a point of diamond: these two implements indicate the permanence of our sin. An iron pen would be used to engrave in stone, while the diamond point would engrave in metal. What other permanent forms of marking might we use today?

The Sin of Judah (17:1–13)

The sins of the people are engraved upon their hearts. The man who turns from the Lord will be like a shrub in the desert. It is better to be like a tree planted beside the water, constantly fed and watered by the Lord.

CLEAR THE CONFUSION

What is meant by the passage "The heart is deceitful above all things, and desperately sick; who can understand it?" (v. 9)?

Our heart is so incurably ill with sin that it deceives us and distorts all our thinking. None of us can understand how sinful we are or the hidden sins of which we are unaware. Only God's Word can make us recognize these.

Jeremiah Prays for Deliverance (17:14–18)

Jeremiah appeals to the Lord for healing and justice against those who oppose him. Rather than being terrorized by the Lord, Jeremiah finds comfort in Him.

Keep the Sabbath Holy (17:19–27)

Jeremiah reminds Judah to set aside their burdens and follow God's Sabbath law. If they honor it, God will preserve the city and the line of David. If they will not, the gates of the city will be consumed.

The Potter and the Clay (18:1–23)

Just as the potter is able to re-create a "spoiled" pot, so the Lord can restore His sin-spoiled people. Jeremiah learns their plans against himself and calls on the Lord to bring down His justice on these faithless Judeans.

VISUALIZE

Why is a broken flask, a container of liquid, a powerful symbol of God's judgment against sinners who will not repent?

The Broken Flask (19:1–15)

Jeremiah is to take a pottery flask to the Potsherd Gate of Jerusalem and pronounce God's judgment against Judah's sin and unfaithfulness, then shatter the flask as the symbol of God's coming wrath.

CLEAR THE CONFUSION

The Potter and the Clay Versus the Broken Flask

Unfired clay can be molded, but the broken flask in Jeremiah 19 has been fired and glazed in the high temperatures of the kiln. This results in a strong but brittle object. Once the flask is shattered, there is no putting it back together.

Jeremiah Persecuted by Pashhur (20:1–18)

Pashhur, a high-ranking administrative priest, beats Jeremiah and puts him in stocks. Jeremiah prophesies that Pashhur's friends will be struck down by the sword and he and his family exiled to Babylon.

Jerusalem Will Fall to Nebuchadnezzar (21:1–10)

King Zedekiah asks Jeremiah to inquire if the Lord will miraculously protect Jerusalem from Nebuchadnezzar's armies. The Lord promises if they surrender, they will live. If they remain in the city, they will die.

Message to the House of David (21:11–22:10)

Jeremiah reminds the descendants of David of their duty as leaders to execute justice and protect their people, especially foreigners, widows, and orphans, from those who would rob or oppress them.

Message to the Sons of Josiah (22:11–30)

Jeremiah sends a message of rebuke against the three kings of Judah who preceded Zedekiah. Unlike Josiah, their father, they focused on personal gain and cared nothing for their citizens. None of them will return.

The Righteous Branch (23:1–8)

What so you expect from our leaders today, both political and religious leaders?

God's message of the righteous Branch can assure and comfort His people. How does God's Word give you confidence in your salvation?

What has God called you to do in your everyday life to serve Him and show care for others?

WAYPOINT

What does this text show us?
The Lord speaks against the sons of David who did not care for His people. The flocks have been scattered and driven away. Soon God will raise up a true "righteous Branch," who will reign as the faithful shepherd over His people.

What does this text reveal about God's plan of salvation?
The Lord will send a righteous Branch to save His people and bring them out of captivity. This righteous Branch is God's own Son, Jesus Christ. He will lead God's people to their eternal home by His death and resurrection.

What does this text uncover about our identity and calling as God's people today?
We are lost sheep who cannot follow the Good Shepherd on our own. The righteous Branch, our Good Shepherd, claims us as His own. In Baptism, He washes away our sin and we dwell secure in our faith, assured of His care for us.

Lying Prophets (23:9–40)

Jeremiah preaches against false prophets who claim to speak for God but whose messages are filled with falsehoods designed to please the people rather than the true God. They will suffer God's punishment.

CLEAR THE CONFUSION

What did it mean that true prophets "stood in the council of the LORD" (v. 18)?

The council of the Lord is the gathering of God's holy angels around Him, listening to His words and receiving His directives. God revealed His Word to His prophets as if they were standing with the angels as part of God's council.

The Good Figs and the Bad Figs (24:1–10)

Jeremiah sees two baskets with good and bad figs. The good figs represent the exiles whom God will restore. The bad figs—King Zedekiah and those who remain in Jerusalem—will be destroyed for their unfaithfulness.

Seventy Years of Captivity (25:1–14)

The Lord warns of punishment and captivity for those in Jerusalem who continue to reject His warnings. The people will be held in exile by Babylon for seventy years until God returns them to their homeland.

The Cup of the LORD's Wrath (25:15–38)

All nations will suffer God's wrath for their sins, thus Jeremiah's message of repentance is for all nations. This is the cup Jesus will drink to the very dregs on the cross to save us from suffering God's wrath in hell.

Jeremiah Threatened with Death (26:1–15)

The priests and false prophets demand that Judah's leaders put Jeremiah to death for prophesying against Jerusalem and the temple. Jeremiah warns them God will hold them guilty if they shed innocent blood.

It is difficult to imagine the stress of Jeremiah's service. Consider those who serve the Lord in our world today. Who might be under similar threat of death for speaking the Gospel?

PICTURE OF THE SAVIOR

Jesus' Life Threatened

Jesus faced death threats from his Nazareth neighbors, the Jewish religious leaders, and the city of Jerusalem. The chief priests, Pharisees, and scribes arrested Jesus and pressured Pilate to crucify Him.

Jeremiah Spared from Death (26:16–24)

The officials spare Jeremiah from death, citing the example of Micah, who prophesied in Hezekiah's time. Hezekiah and the people heeded Micah's words and repented, and Judah was delivered from the Assyrians.

Ahikam's father, Shaphan, had been a trusted official of faithful King Josiah. Ahikam's son Gedaliah will be appointed governor after Jerusalem falls, only to be assassinated by princes of the house of David (see Jeremiah 41). What faithful servants of God have you seen oppressed and persecuted?

VISUALIZE

The Yoke of Nebuchadnezzar (27:1–22)

Jeremiah wears an animal yoke and proclaims that those nations who yoke or subject themselves to the Babylonians will remain in their land. Those who refuse will be struck down with war and famine.

VISUALIZE

What is a yoke?

Yokes connect donkeys, horses, and oxen to heavy equipment like plows or wagons. The yoke helps distribute heavy loads in order to make the task easier for the animal. Many yokes were designed to be used by animals working in pairs in order to perform difficult tasks.

Hananiah the False Prophet (28:1–17)

The false prophet Hananiah breaks Jeremiah's yoke. He declares the temple vessels, King Jeconiah, and the exiles will return within two years. Because of this false prophecy, Hananiah dies that same year.

Christians frequently quote Jeremiah 29:11, "For I know the plans I have for you, declares the LORD, plans for welfare and not for evil, to give you a future and a hope." How did this verse comfort the people at the time of Jeremiah? How can it comfort believers today?

Jeremiah's Letter to the Exiles (29:1–23)

Jeremiah writes a letter to King Jeconiah and those in Babylon. Their exile will last seventy years. So they should settle down and raise families and seek the welfare of the places they live so it may go well with them.

Shemaiah's False Prophecy (29:24–32)

Shemaiah, a false prophet exiled in Babylon, claims God made him a priest. He accuses Jeremiah of being a madman who needs to be locked in stocks and neck irons. Jeremiah sends a letter condemning Shemaiah.

Restoration for Israel and Judah (30:1–24)

Jeremiah pauses in the middle of his book to include sweet, comforting Gospel for that remnant of people whose heart God has touched, who are truly repentant and grieve to see the evil all around them.

The LORD Will Turn Mourning to Joy (31:1–30)

The people will be exiled for seventy years. When their exile ends, God will return them to the Promised Land. The divided nations of Israel and Judah will once again be united. They all will worship the one true God.

LINK BETWEEN THE TESTAMENTS

Rachel Weeping for Her Children → Herod Kills the Children (Jeremiah 31:15 → Matthew 2:16–18)

Rachel died in childbirth when Jacob was leading his family toward Bethlehem; he buried her in Ramah. Jeremiah portrayed Rachel at Ramah, weeping over the descendants of her son Benjamin as they're taken into captivity with Judah.

Rachel's tears foreshadowed the tears of parents mourning their sons whom ruthless King Herod ordered slaughtered when the Wise Men did not report Jesus' location to him.

The New Covenant (31:31–40)

WAYPOINT

What do you think it means that God will write His Law on His people's hearts?

How has Jesus transformed our relationship with God, our Father?

God's plan of salvation does not depend on our works. How is this great news for you as a recipient of God's grace?

What does this text show us?
The Lord will establish a new covenant with His people, one not based on the Law of Moses given at Mount Sinai. He will put His Law within them and write it on their hearts. Jerusalem will be rebuilt as the people return from exile.

What does this text reveal about God's plan of salvation?
God's new covenant with His people will be written on their hearts, a covenant built on God's grace through faith. Through Jesus' perfect, sinless life, our sins are forgiven and we inherit eternal life with the Lord through faith.

What does this text uncover about our identity and calling as God's people today?
Although we live in a world opposed to God, Christ is with us. He has gone ahead to prepare a home for all believers. Just as Jerusalem would be rebuilt for the Israelites, so He is building the new Jerusalem as our eternal home.

Jeremiah Buys a Field During the Siege (32:1–15)

Though imprisoned in Jerusalem by King Zedekiah, Jeremiah sends his cousin Hanamel to purchase a field to show his faith that the Lord will keep His promise to return His people to buy and sell homes in the land.

Jeremiah Prays for Understanding (32:16–35)

Jeremiah does not understand the reason for the purchase. God explains why the city is under siege and will be destroyed, especially the places where false worship took place, even on people's rooftops.

What does it mean for you to be part of God's chosen people? How do we become His children?

They Shall Be My People; I Will Be Their God (32:36–44)

Jerusalem will fall to Babylon. But God will gather His people from all the places where they will be scattered. The "great disaster" (v. 42) will lead to restoration. God will make them His people for all eternity.

The LORD Promises Peace (33:1–13)

Jeremiah describes panic as houses are torn down to fill gaps in Jerusalem's walls. Jeremiah despairs over the abandoned city and desolate fields. But God promises Jerusalem will once again be filled with people and flocks.

The LORD's Eternal Covenant with David (33:14–26)

From David's house, God will raise up a righteous Branch to rule Israel forever. Jesus will be both our King and our High Priest, offering Himself upon the cross. And He will make all believers royal priests, offering our prayers and good works to God.

Zedekiah to Die in Babylon (34:1–22)

The book of comfort is completed, and we now return to God's judgment upon Judah. Jeremiah tells King Zedekiah that he will die in Babylon. There will not be glorious death in battle but in exile, far from home.

The Obedience of the Rechabites (35:1–19)

The Lord instructs Jeremiah to bring the Rechabites to the temple. They refuse wine because one ancestor ordered their generations to avoid it. Their obedience should make Israel ashamed for not obeying God's voice.

Jeremiah's Suffering and Persecution (36:1–38:28)

These three chapters focus on the suffering Jeremiah endured from the kings, priests, and people in Jerusalem and Judah who failed to repent of their sins.

The description of Jehoiakim cutting off portions of the scroll as they are read and then burning them reflects his arrogant attitude. How can our arrogance toward God lead us into sinful behavior?

Jehoiakim Burns Jeremiah's Scroll (36:1–32)

Jeremiah records all of God's judgments against Israel on a scroll. As the scroll is read to King Jehoiakim, he cuts it up and burns up the entire scroll. Then the Lord instructs Jeremiah to write a second scroll.

Jeremiah Warns Zedekiah (37:1–10)

When Nebuchadnezzar breaks the siege of Jerusalem to engage the Egyptian armies, Jeremiah tells Zedekiah the Egyptians will fail and the Chaldeans will return and burn Jerusalem with fire.

Jeremiah Imprisoned (37:11–21)

When Zedekiah brings Jeremiah from prison for a private audience, Jeremiah reminds him the false prophets said Babylon would never attack, but now their army surrounds Jerusalem. Zedekiah moves Jeremiah to the court of the guard.

Jeremiah Cast into the Cistern (38:1–6)

The officials accuse Jeremiah of treason when he advises people to surrender to the Chaldeans. King Zedekiah allows them to throw Jeremiah into an empty water cistern.

Consider the risk the men who rescued Jeremiah were taking. What might have happened to them? Who takes a similar risk to help others in our world today?

Jeremiah Rescued from the Cistern (38:7–13)

Ebed-melech, a servant in the king's household, begs Zedekiah to rescue Jeremiah. The king gives him thirty men and they rescue the prophet. Jeremiah stays in the court of the guard after that.

CLEAR THE CONFUSION

Why did King Zedekiah authorize Jeremiah's rescue?

Zedekiah was actually a weak king. He listened closely to the warnings Jeremiah gave him but was afraid to obey the Lord and stand up to his wicked officials.

Jeremiah Warns Zedekiah Again (38:14–28)

Jeremiah warns Zedekiah to surrender like Jehoiachin. If he does, his life will be spared and the city will not be burned. But if he refuses, his wives and sons will be exiled, the city will be destroyed, and he will die in Babylon.

The Fall of Jerusalem (39:1–45:5)

Jeremiah chronicles the events surrounding the fall of Jerusalem.

You can read more about the destruction of Jerusalem in 2 Kings 25:1–21. Why do you suppose the Babylonians carried away so many of the temple furnishings?

The Fall of Jerusalem (39:1–10)

Zedekiah is captured, watches his sons get slaughtered, then is blinded and dragged to Babylon in chains. The temple, the king's house, and the people's houses are burned down. Jerusalem's walls are torn down.

CLEAR THE CONFUSION

Who got to stay behind?

Judah's poorest people, who owned no land of their own, were to care for the vineyards, fields, and flocks. These poor citizens were likely already fulfilling these tasks for wealthier landowners now exiled or killed.

The LORD Delivers Jeremiah (39:11–18)

Jeremiah is released and entrusted to Gedaliah, who is appointed governor of the remnant in Judah. As a result of his faith and trust in the Lord, Jeremiah is spared from the sword and from exile.

Jeremiah chose to remain in Judah. Why do you suppose he made this choice?

Jeremiah Remains in Judah (40:1–16)

Jeremiah stays in Judah with Gedaliah. Survivors from Judah's army join Gedaliah in Mizpah. Gedaliah is warned of an assassination plot against him but refuses to believe it.

Gedaliah Murdered (41:1–18)

Ishmael strikes down Gedaliah, the governor, with the sword then flees. Afraid the Chaldeans will take revenge for Gedaliah's murder, Johanan prepares to flee to Egypt with the remaining Israelites.

Warning Against Going to Egypt (42:1–22)

Johanan seeks the Lord's guidance from Jeremiah, promising to obey however the Lord answers. Jeremiah warns him if they flee to Egypt they will all die. He urges them to remain in Judah and trust in God's mercy.

Why do you think Johanan and his men refused to obey Jeremiah's message? How do you react when someone ignores your godly advice?

Jeremiah, the faithful prophet, exposed the unrepentance of the Jews who fled to Egypt, then he was killed. How does Jeremiah's ministry illustrate God's reckless love for His people and foreshadow Jesus' coming death?

Jeremiah Taken to Egypt (43:1–13)

Johanan disobeys God and takes Jeremiah and the remnant to Egypt. Jeremiah hides two large stones before Pharaoh's palace because Nebuchadnezzar will set his throne over these stones and rule over Egypt.

Judgment for Idolatry (44:1–30)

The Israelites claim they prospered in Manasseh's days, but after they stopped serving the star goddess (see 7:18) everything went wrong. Jeremiah delivers his last recorded message.

Message to Baruch (45:1–5)

God tells Jeremiah's scribe Baruch that despite his faithfulness, he will experience some of the same pains the people will experience. Baruch should trust God to protect him through the coming trials.

Judgment Against the Nations (46:1–51:64)

Jeremiah lists God's judgment upon the Gentile nations that surround Israel. Judgment begins with the people of God but extends over all the earth. This is a powerful reminder of Christ's return on the Last Day.

SET THE SCENE

Judgment Against the Nations

Chapters 46–51 contain a series of judgments against the nations of the world, most of which would be considered enemies of God's chosen people in Palestine.

VISUALIZE

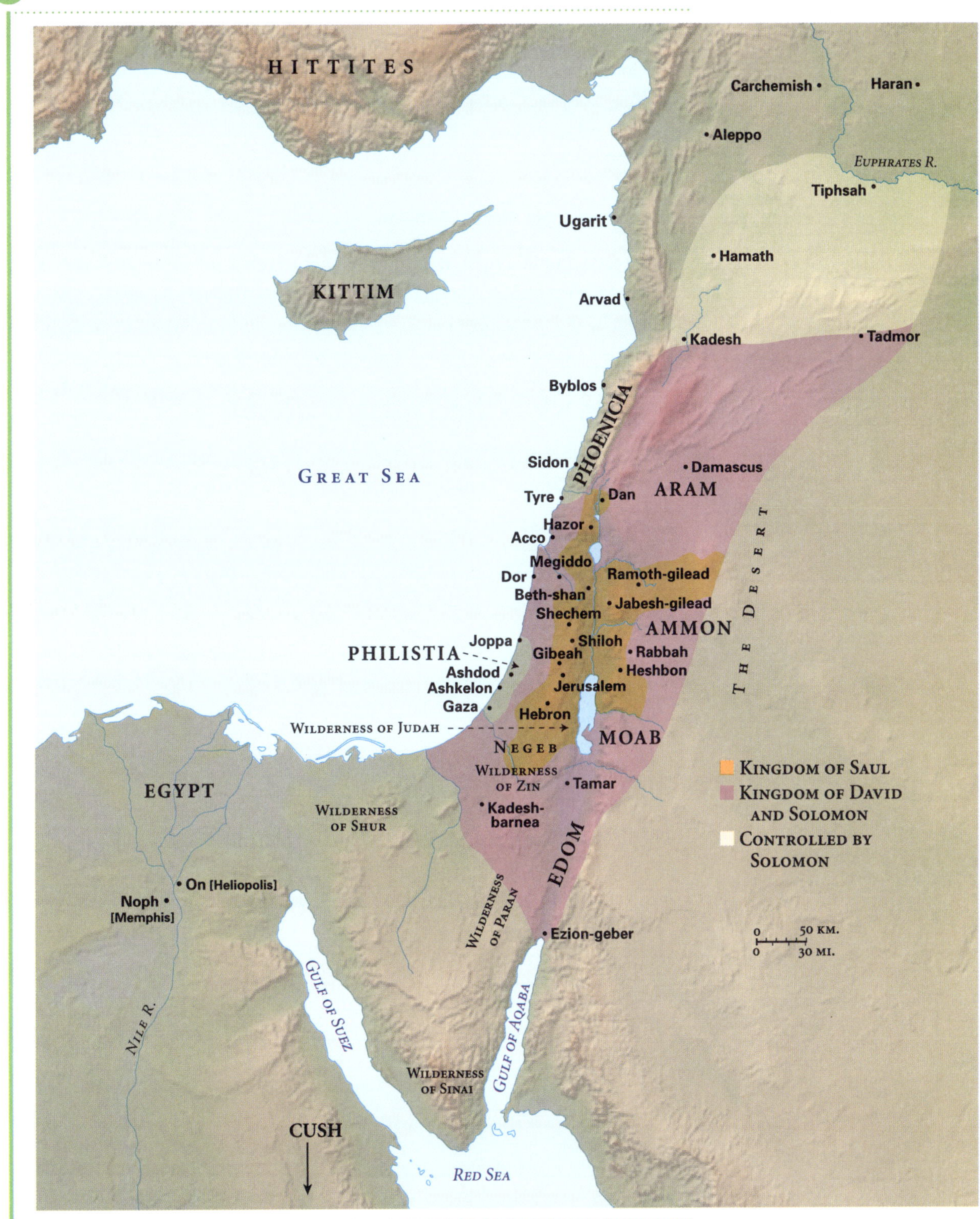

HITTITES
Carchemish
Haran
Aleppo
Euphrates R.
Tiphsah
Ugarit
Hamath
KITTIM
Arvad
Kadesh
Tadmor
Byblos
PHOENICIA
Sidon
Damascus
Great Sea
Tyre
Dan
ARAM
Hazor
Acco
Megiddo
Dor
Ramoth-gilead
Beth-shan
Jabesh-gilead
Shechem
The Desert
AMMON
Joppa
Shiloh
PHILISTIA
Gibeah
Rabbah
Ashdod
Heshbon
Ashkelon
Jerusalem
Gaza
Hebron
Wilderness of Judah
MOAB
Negeb
Wilderness of Zin
Tamar
Kingdom of Saul
Kingdom of David and Solomon
Controlled by Solomon
EGYPT
Wilderness of Shur
Kadesh-barnea
EDOM
On [Heliopolis]
Noph [Memphis]
Wilderness of Paran
Ezion-geber
0 50 km.
0 30 mi.
Gulf of Suez
Gulf of Aqaba
Nile R.
Wilderness of Sinai
CUSH
Red Sea

Judgment on Egypt (46:1–28)

Jeremiah describes Egypt's defeat by the Babylonians at Carchemish. Following that, Nebuchadnezzar invades Egypt because they have given refuge to the remnant from Judah who promised to remain in Judah.

SET THE SCENE

Egypt's Struggle Against Babylon

After Assyria fell, Egypt and Babylon vied to replace it. Though losing at Carchemish in 605 BC, Egypt continued pestering Babylon by alliances with Judah, Ammon, and other nations. Finally, Nebuchadnezzar conquered Egypt.

Judgment on the Philistines (47:1–7)

Through Jeremiah, God declares His judgment on the Philistines. Through a people from the north, God will destroy the Philistines.

SET THE SCENE

The Philistines

The Philistines came from the Aegean Sea. They attacked coastal cities then finally settled on the Mediterranean coast of Canaan. When Israel entered the Promised Land, the Philistines were entrenched and difficult to drive out.

What other nations have experienced complete destruction because they chose to ignore God's direction?

Judgment on Moab (48:1–47)

Moab held Israel in derision and celebrated Israel's defeat. The image of Moab being poured out and her jars broken to pieces reflects the vineyards and wine industry for which Moab was known.

Judgment on Ammon (49:1–6)

When Nebuchadnezzar set Gedaliah as governor over Judah, the king of the Ammonites joined the assassination conspiracy (see 40:13–41:15). God threatens destruction for their hostility toward His people.

Judgment on Edom (49:7–22)

The descendants of Esau angered God by their great hostility toward Israel. As a result, they will face God's destructive wrath. Jeremiah uses a vineyard metaphor to describe the coming judgment on Edom.

As you read each of these judgments, what common themes do you notice?

Judgment on Damascus (49:23–27)

Damascus, the capital city of Syria (Aram), had long opposed God's chosen people (see 1 and 2 Kings). God judges Damascus to protect His people and turn the Syrians from their false gods.

Judgment on Kedar and Hazor (49:28–33)

Kedar and Hazor were two unwalled villages that were defenseless against Nebuchadnezzar's forces. Their ancestor was Ishmael, Abraham's son through Sarah's slave Hagar. They are not able to avoid God's judgment.

Judgment on Elam (49:34–39)

Elam had supported Babylon's attacks on Judah. The Elamites will be scattered to the four corners of the earth. Yet later, Jews from Elam are part of the Pentecost crowds in Acts 2.

SET THE SCENE

The End Before the Beginning

Jeremiah's prophetic oracles against the nations conclude with the destruction of Babylon, the tool God had used to punish all the other nations before it. Note how Jeremiah spoke about the destruction in the past tense.

Judgment on Babylon (50:1–46)

God carried out His justice on Judah and Jerusalem through the Babylonians. But He will still bring destruction upon Babylon because of their arrogance and sinful attitude against God and against His people.

CLEAR THE CONFUSION

How soon were the exiles permitted to return home after Babylon fell to Cyrus the Persian?

Ezra records Cyrus's proclamation permitting the Jews to return to Jerusalem in the first year of his reign (see Ezra 1:1).

The Utter Destruction of Babylon (51:1–64)

The judgment on Babylon is coming and God desires to spare His people from the dangers in Babylon. This lengthy chapter portrays the complete nature of the destruction Babylon will face.

Historical Appendix (52:1–34)

Chapter 51 ends with the words "Thus far are the words of Jeremiah." The final chapter of Jeremiah is a historical account that shows all the prophecies of Jeremiah had been accurate.

The Fall of Jerusalem Recounted (52:1–11)

In the ninth year of Zedekiah's reign, Nebuchadnezzar begins a siege of Jerusalem that lasts two years. Zedekiah sees the wall has been breached and attempts to escape, but he is captured. He dies imprisoned in Babylon.

Jesus likened this destruction of the temple to His suffering and death on the cross. How would the rebuilding of the temple when the exiles returned parallel Jesus' resurrection on the third day?

The Temple Burned (52:12–23)

Jeremiah describes the destruction of the temple, the city walls, and other Jerusalem buildings. The Chaldean army carries off the bronze pillars, the various implements, and all the major furnishings from the temple.

The People Exiled to Babylon (52:24–30)

In 605 BC, when Jehoiakim reigned, 3,023 Judeans were exiled to Babylon (including Daniel, Shadrach, Meshach, and Abednego). Seven years later, in 598, when his son Jehoiachin surrendered, 832 persons were taken into exile (including Ezekiel). Finally, eleven years later in 587, when Zedekiah is defeated, Nebuchadnezzar exiles 745 persons.

Jehoiachin Released from Prison (52:31–34)

Thirty-seven years after Jerusalem's fall, King Nebuchadnezzar dies and his son Evil-merodach becomes king. Evil-merodach releases Jehoiachin from captivity and gives him a place of honor at the king's table.

LAMENTATIONS

Welcome to Lamentations

The book of Lamentations consists of five poems of grief and lamenting written by the prophet Jeremiah. They represent the suffering and grief the people of Jerusalem experienced during the siege and the exile to Babylon. Each chapter is a separate poem. The center poem in chapter 3 is more hope- and grace-filled than the preceding and following poems. As you read Lamentations, consider dark times in your life and the blessing of having these God-given prayers through which you can pour out your grief and sorrow to your Lord and Savior.

What do you think about complaining to God in your prayers? What is appropriate to complain about and what is not?

Lamentations at a Glance

- **Start:** Lamentations starts after the Babylonian exile. Once thriving and full of people, Jerusalem now sits desolate and empty.
- **End:** Lamentations ends with a poem of repentance and confession and a desperate plea to God to restore His people.
- **Theme:** Lamentations focuses on contrition, repentance, and sorrow as the Lord pours out His judgment on Judah.
- **Author and Date:** The five chapters of Lamentations were written by the prophet Jeremiah in 587 BC at the fall of Jerusalem.
- **Places Visited:** Jerusalem, Judah, and Israel
- **Journey Time:** The five chapters of Lamentations can be read in approximately twenty minutes.
- **Outline:**
    - The Misery of Jerusalem (1:1–22)
    - The Lord's Anger (2:1–22)
    - The Lord's Discipline and Mercy (3:1–66)
    - Zion's Punishment (4:1–22)
    - A Plea to the Lord (5:1–22)

Five Top Sights and Spectacles of Lamentations

A Lonely City (1:1–4) Experience the desolation of Jerusalem as she faces a future of abandonment.

The Lord Shows No Pity (2:1–3) Look on in sorrow as the Lord carries out His righteous judgment.

The Lord's Great Faithfulness (3:21–24) Amid destruction and sorrow, witness the promise of the Lord's great mercy on His people.

Scattered Stones (4:1) Step carefully through the ruins of Jerusalem and the Lord's temple.

Restore Us, O Lord (5:21) Add your voice to the prophet who calls out to God in the midst of seemingly endless destruction.

Seeing Jesus in Lamentations

The five poems of lament remind us of Jesus' cry on the cross, "My God, My God, why have You forsaken Me?" (Matthew 27:46). Yet they trust God to restore His exiled people, just as Jesus trusted God to raise Him from the dead.

The Misery of Jerusalem (1:1–22)

Jeremiah's description of the empty city of Jerusalem contains a number of images. What do these images remind you of?

How Lonely Sits the City (1:1–22)

Jerusalem is like a humiliated, deserted widow. Mocked and ridiculed by her enemies, she prays for God to punish them for their sins, as Jeremiah had promised in his prophecies against the nations (Jeremiah 46–51).

SET THE SCENE

Widows in the Ancient World

Comparing barren Jerusalem to a widow would have been easily understood in ancient Israel. Women had no property rights and completely depended on their husband or sons. Childless widows could only beg for others' charity.

PICTURE OF THE SAVIOR

Good Friday Liturgy

The Good Friday liturgy incorporates Lamentations 1:12: "Is it nothing to you, all you who pass by? Look and see if there is any sorrow like My sorrow, which was brought upon Me, which the LORD inflicted on the day of His fierce anger."

The Lord's Anger (2:1–22)

The Lord Has Destroyed Without Pity (2:1–22)

The second poem laments how the Lord showed no pity when He punished Jerusalem's idolatry and wickedness. The poem calls on the people to cry out to God in repentance and to plead for His mercy.

Why is it difficult to understand the destruction God brings upon the city of Jerusalem?

CLEAR THE CONFUSION

Why was God so angry?

After sending so many prophets to call on His people to repent, the Lord finally allowed Jerusalem's destruction. We, too, deserve God's punishment of hell for our sins. But God rescued us by punishing His Son, Jesus, in our place.

The Lord's Discipline and Mercy (3:1–66)

Great Is Your Faithfulness (3:1–66)

VISUALIZE

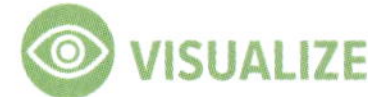

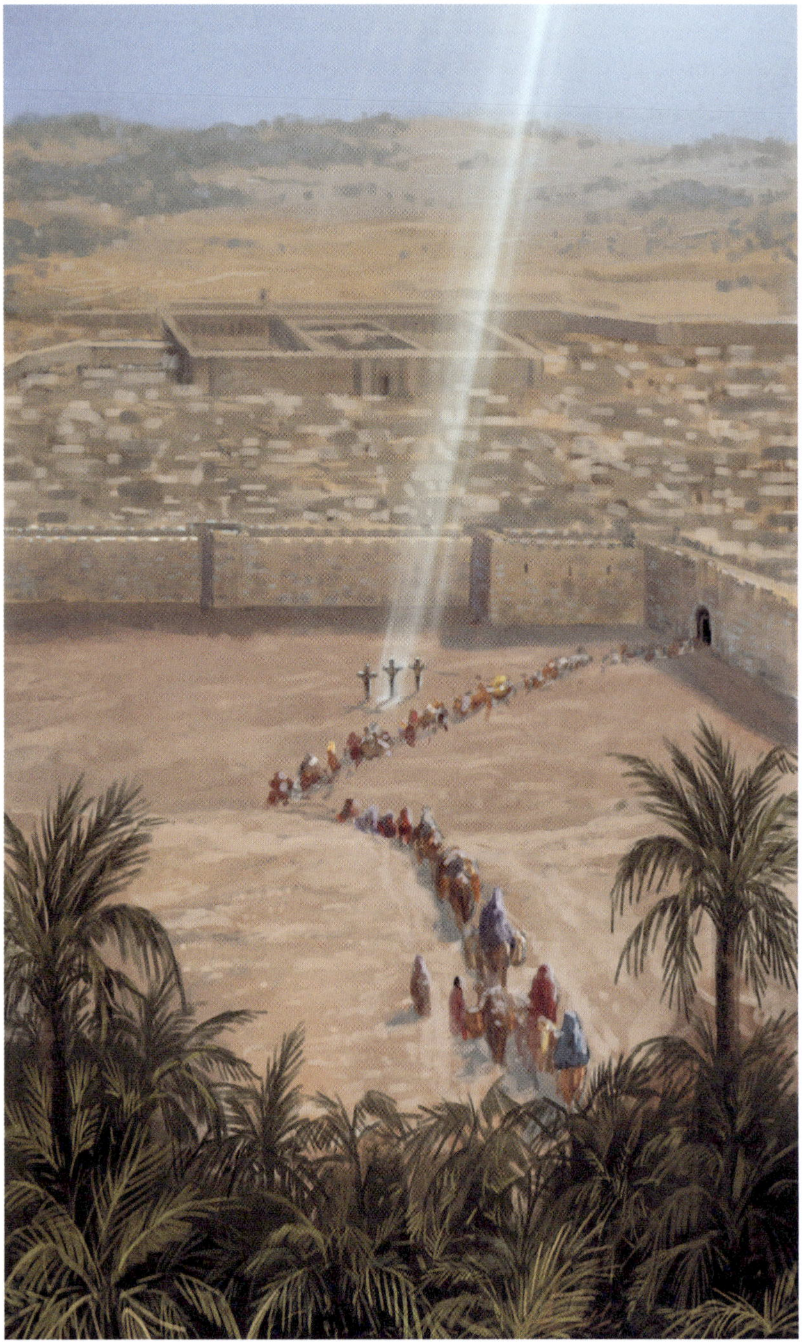

WAYPOINT

What does this text show us?
The third song discusses the people's suffering then recounts God's loving mercy. After assuring us God does not delight in our sufferings, Jeremiah reminds us that the Lord will defend us from those who reject Him.

What does this text reveal about God's plan of salvation?
Through Jesus, God will rescue His people. The Lord has overcome our enemies and defends His followers. The Lord is loving and compassionate, remaining faithful even when we sin repeatedly. We can trust in the Lord at all times.

What does this text uncover about our identity and calling as God's people today?
We live in the fulfillment of His promise to rescue His chosen people from their enemies. We live in a world hostile to our faith and beliefs and daily face these challenges. We can trust in the Lord to defend us from all evil.

What part of this lament do you most relate to? Why?

God's plan of salvation does not depend on our works. How is this great news for you as a recipient of God's grace?

What comfort do you see in God's promises to defend His people from their enemies?

Zion's Punishment (4:1–22)

The Holy Stones Lie Scattered (4:1–22)

This poem teaches us to cry out to the Lord so we recognize our sins are the reason we suffer, not God being cruel. In the end, God removes any resentment toward Him and brings us peace as He restores us.

CLEAR THE CONFUSION

Why did God compare the Israelites to ostriches in the wilderness (v. 3)?

In their starvation and misery, Israel's mothers abandoned their children. Thus the mothers in Jerusalem were like ostriches who lay their eggs but then abandon the chicks. Sometimes ostriches even trample and destroy their eggs.

SET THE SCENE

The Destruction of Jerusalem

The Chaldeans tore down Jerusalem's walls, plundered the wealth of Solomon's temple, and set the temple and city ablaze. The survivors who remained with Gedaliah the governor were unable to live in Jerusalem. They moved to Mizpah.

A Plea to the Lord (5:1–22)

How has God restored us as His people?

Restore Us to Yourself, O LORD (5:1–22)

The once-celebrated chosen ones have fallen from their elevated status. Jeremiah closes this last lament pleading for the Lord to restore His people and put aside His anger toward them.

CLEAR THE CONFUSION

What does "We get our bread at the peril of our lives, because of the sword in the wilderness" mean (v. 9)?

The survivors in Judea were the victims of Bedouin raiders, who came through the land to loot what they wanted. It was much like life during the time of the judges, when Israel was subjugated under other nations.

LINK BETWEEN THE TESTAMENTS

The Lord Reigns Forever → The Kingdom Comes → The Alpha and the Omega (Lamentations 5:19 → Luke 17:20–21 → Revelation 22:12–13)

Jeremiah's final lament ends with his assertion that the Lord's kingdom will last forever. This statement seemed impossible at the time, with the city of Jerusalem and Solomon's great temple lying in ruins.

Jesus assured His disciples He was among them to establish His everlasting spiritual kingdom, first through His New Testament church then after Judgment Day throughout the new heavens and the new earth.

In the closing verses of Scripture, John proclaims Jesus Christ as the Alpha and the Omega, the beginning and the end, the one for whom there is no end. He alone is the Lord who will reign forever.

EZEKIEL

Welcome to Ezekiel

What do you know about the book of Ezekiel? What are you hoping to learn?

Ezekiel was a priest exiled to Babylon in 597 BC when King Jehoiachin surrendered to Nebuchadnezzar, king of Babylon. In this book, God calls Ezekiel to be the prophet to his fellow exiles.

Since Nebuchadnezzar had spared the temple at this time, the exiles believe they will return home soon. Ezekiel warns them God will destroy the city and the temple because of the idolatry still taking place there. When the temple is finally destroyed, they lose all hope. Ezekiel promises them God will bring them back and send the Messiah.

As you read Ezekiel, you will encounter strange images and visions, much like those in the book of Revelation. Keep in mind that the whole book is about God's punishment of sins and His mercy and grace through Jesus Christ, who has paid for all those sins on the cross.

Ezekiel at a Glance

- **Start:** Ezekiel sees the glory of God by the Chebar canal in Babylon.
- **End:** Ezekiel takes a guided tour of the new temple in Jerusalem.
- **Theme:** God's glory has departed from Israel because of their sin, but He will restore His people and return to dwell with them.
- **Author and Date:** Ezekiel the priest and prophet wrote this book between 593 and 570 BC.
- **Places Visited:** Babylon, Chebar canal, Jerusalem, Israel, Judah, the temple of Jerusalem, Ammon, Moab, and others
- **Journey Time:** Ezekiel's forty-eight chapters can be read in about four hours.
- **Outline:**
  - Ezekiel's Call (1:1–7:27)
  - God's Glory Abandons the Jerusalem Temple (8:1–11:25)
  - Oracles of Judgment on Israel (12:1–24:27)
  - Oracles Against Other Nations (25:1–32:32)
  - Oracles and Visions of Israel's Restoration (33:1–48:35)

Five Top Sights and Spectacles of Ezekiel

The Glory of the Lord (1:4–28) Watch in wonder as the God of Israel appears in glory to Ezekiel by a canal in Babylon.

Ezekiel's Call (2:1–10) Taste the sweet Gospel in the scroll Ezekiel eats, but feel it turn sour in your stomach because of Israel's sin.

The Glory of the Lord Leaves the Temple (10:1–22) Follow the cloud of the Lord's glory as it departs from the temple and city.

The Valley of Dry Bones (37:1–14) Feel the power of the Holy Spirit as an army of dry bones is resurrected.

The Glory of the Lord Fills the Temple (43:1–12) Tour the new temple with Ezekiel and watch the glory of the Lord fill it.

Seeing Jesus in Ezekiel

The preincarnate Christ commissions Ezekiel in the first chapter. He speaks through Ezekiel to condemn the sins that doom Solomon's temple and to convict the exiles of their own sin and guilt, which have brought them into exile. Christ promises to give them new, faithful hearts and to dwell among them as their great prince and faithful shepherd forever.

Ezekiel's Call (1:1–7:27)

God calls Ezekiel to be His messenger to the exiles in Babylon. Ezekiel exposes the sins of those who remain in Jerusalem with the temple. He prophesies the temple's destruction and another deportation of Judeans.

How do you think a person knows if God is calling him or her to full-time service in the church?

Ezekiel in Babylon (1:1–3)

Instead of serving as a priest in the Jerusalem temple, Ezekiel begins his ministry in exile. God comes to Babylon in great glory to commission him as prophet while he stands among the exiles by the Chebar canal.

SET THE SCENE

Who was King Jehoiachin?

Jehoiachin was the unfaithful grandson of faithful King Josiah. Jehoiachin surrendered when Nebuchadnezzar besieged Jerusalem. Through him and his descendants, the line of David continued to Jesus Christ.

Why is it important to remember Jesus in His glorious splendor as well as His lowly humanity?

The Glory of the LORD (1:4–28)

Ezekiel sees four heavenly creatures and their wheels, which form a square vehicle carrying God's throne. The preincarnate Christ has come on this throne in great glory to commission Ezekiel as His prophet.

VISUALIZE

CLEAR THE CONFUSION

What was the significance of this glorious appearance of the Lord?

By appearing in His great power and glory here in the land of Babylon, God reminded the exiles that He rules the entire heavens and the earth that He created—yes, even the pagan Babylonian Empire.

Ezekiel's Call (2:1–3:15)

WAYPOINT

What does this text show us?
Christ warns Ezekiel the people of Israel are a stiff-necked, stubborn, and rebellious house. Ezekiel is to speak all the words the Lord gives him and be as stubborn in proclaiming this word as the people are in not believing it.

What does this text reveal about God's plan of salvation?
During Jesus' ministry, people thronged around to hear His gracious words, but few believed His message. He stubbornly set His face to go up to Jerusalem to die for our salvation. Jesus still offers His steadfast love and mercy to all.

What does this text uncover about our identity and calling as God's people today?
Each of us is conceived a sinner, stubborn and hard-hearted against the Lord. But the Holy Spirit works through God's Word to bring us to repentance and faith. Throughout our lives, the Spirit molds us into the image of Christ.

Where does the sinful stubbornness of people come from?

Why is it to our advantage that God is stubborn about our repentance and salvation?

What are some situations in your life when you find you are being stubborn and having a hard time trusting God's Word?

A Watchman for Israel (3:16–27)

God makes Ezekiel a watchman for Israel. He must warn Judah of God's approaching wrath so they can repent and be saved. If Ezekiel warns the people but they don't listen, their blood is on their own hands.

The Siege of Jerusalem Symbolized (4:1–17)

God tells Ezekiel to act out the siege of Jerusalem. Ezekiel lies on his side eating bread and water, just as the inhabitants of Jerusalem will do when the Babylonian armies surround and trap them in Jerusalem.

What value would a visible representation of the siege of Jerusalem have for the exiles? Is your preferred learning style visual or auditory?

SET THE SCENE

Why did God give Ezekiel these action prophecies?

By acting out these prophecies, Ezekiel made them more memorable, more powerful. He let the exiles visualize what was happening back in Jerusalem.

Jerusalem Will Be Destroyed (5:1–17)

Ezekiel is to shave his hair and beard to depict the capture of Jerusalem, the burning of the city and the temple, the death of many Jews by the sword, and the exile of the rest. But God will graciously spare a remnant.

Judgment Against Idolatry (6:1–14)

Ezekiel prophesies against the mountains of Israel where the Israelites had built high places to false gods. Those high places will be destroyed, and those who offer sacrifices there will be killed and denied proper burial.

The Day of the Wrath of the LORD (7:1–27)

The Babylonian siege will bring the sword to those outside Jerusalem's walls and famine and pestilence to those within. The Babylonians will enter their houses and their holy places, looting even the temple itself.

LINK BETWEEN THE TESTAMENTS

The Day of the Wrath of the Lord → Woe to You (Ezekiel 7 → Matthew 23)

Ezekiel warned of the day of God's wrath when Jerusalem would fall and the enemy would wreak God's vengeance. Jesus warned that the Roman armies would break through Jerusalem's walls and burn the temple to the ground.

The exiles set their hopes on the temple rather than the word of God calling them to repent of their sins and trust in His salvation. Where are you tempted to set your hopes rather than on the promise of God in Jesus?

God's Glory Abandons the Jerusalem Temple (8:1–11:25)

When Solomon dedicated the temple, God's glory filled it (1 Kings 8:10–11). Now, because Israel's sins are so great, God withdraws His glory from the temple, making it defenseless against Judah's enemies.

Abominations in the Temple (8:1–18)

The likeness of Christ appears to Ezekiel again, and in a vision, the Holy Spirit takes him to the Jerusalem temple to show him four scenes in which Israelites are committing idolatry and stirring God's wrath.

Idolaters Killed (9:1–11)

The Lord sends six destroyers to kill all the idolaters in Jerusalem but first marks all those who are true believers so they will be spared. The Lord's glory begins to rise from the cover of the ark.

The Glory of the LORD Leaves the Temple (10:1–22)

VISUALIZE

How do you think the exiles responded when Ezekiel shared this vision with them? How should they have responded?

What does this passage teach us about God's mercy and grace?

How often are you conscious of God's protecting presence in your life? How can you cultivate a deeper awareness that He is always with you?

WAYPOINT

What does this text show us?

The preincarnate Christ sits on His throne above the cherubim. The cloud of glory passes through the temple door and threshold, then exits the temple complex through the east gate. The temple now stands forsaken and unprotected.

What does this text reveal about God's plan of salvation?

Though Israel rejects God, He still loves them and calls Ezekiel to serve those in exile. Ultimately, God shows His love for us by forsaking His Son, who bore our sins on the cross, then raising Him from the dead to give us eternal life.

What does this text uncover about our identity and calling as God's people today?

God calls us to repent and empowers us to turn from willful sins. Washed in Jesus' blood and filled with the Holy Spirit, we are empowered by God to share the good news of salvation with other sinners who are caught in their sin.

SET THE SCENE

The Cherubim

In Solomon's temple, there were two cherubim on the cover of the ark and two overshadowing the ark (1 Kings 8:6–7). These match the four cherubim Ezekiel saw and the four living creatures in Revelation 4:6–8.

When the prophet told King Jehoiachin to surrender, it took a lot of trust to obey. What do you find most difficult about trusting God's promises and directions for your life?

Judgment on Wicked Counselors (11:1–13)

At the temple's east gate, Ezekiel sees twenty-five men who assumed leadership over Jerusalem after Jehoiachin's exile. Since they killed their adversaries, they will be taken from the city and judged at Israel's border.

Israel's New Heart and Spirit (11:14–25)

Ezekiel sees the glory of the Lord depart from Jerusalem completely, then tells the exiles God has forsaken the temple but has come to dwell with them. He is their sanctuary in their exile.

CLEAR THE CONFUSION

What is a heart of stone and a heart of flesh?

A heart of stone describes a sinner who refuses to repent. Think of Pharaoh's hardened heart in the exodus account. A heart of flesh hears God's Word, repents of sins, and believes God's promise of forgiveness for Jesus' sake.

Oracles of Judgment on Israel (12:1–24:27)

The Lord keeps shattering the exiles' delusion that Jerusalem will stand and they will soon return to their homes in Jerusalem and Judah. In 587 BC, Jerusalem would finally fall and the temple would be destroyed.

Judah's Captivity Symbolized (12:1–28)

In the sight of the exiles, Ezekiel prepares an exile's baggage, digs through the wall, and carries it out on his shoulder. Ezekiel tells them the princes and people in Jerusalem will be captured and taken into exile.

False Prophets Condemned (13:1–23)

False prophets claim Jerusalem will experience peace instead of violence and destruction. Their prophecies will come to nothing when Babylon captures Jerusalem, loots the temple, and burns it to the ground.

Idolatrous Elders Condemned (14:1–11)

Some elders come to Ezekiel to inquire of God. Since they cling to false gods, Ezekiel tells them God will not answer their inquiry except by judgment. He warns them against trusting false prophets.

Jerusalem Will Not Be Spared (14:12–23)

God's judgment on Jerusalem is inevitable. Nothing can spare it any longer. Even if Noah, Job, and Daniel were present, they could save no one but themselves—not even their sons and daughters.

Jerusalem could no longer be saved but only individuals who heard and believed God's word from Ezekiel. Peter carried this idea when he said, "Save yourselves from this crooked generation" (Acts 2:40). How is the same thing true of the world in which we live?

 **LINK BETWEEN THE TESTAMENTS**

Jerusalem Will Not Be Spared → Each by Grace Through Faith (Ezekiel 14:12–23 → Ephesians 2:1–10)

The righteous faith of Noah, Job, and Daniel could not spare Jerusalem from God's wrath. But God credits Jesus' righteousness to all who believe in Him, and His righteousness is enough to save us in the final judgment.

Jerusalem, a Useless Vine (15:1–8)

The inhabitants of Jerusalem think they are better than the exiles. God compares these inhabitants to a vine growing in a forest. No one can make anything valuable from the soft, pliable wood.

The LORD's Faithless Bride (16:1–58)

God shows Israel's shocking disloyalty by comparing them to an abandoned baby girl He raised to become His queen, only for her to reject Him by her wanton adultery and treachery. This stirs His terrifying wrath.

 **PICTURE OF THE SAVIOR**

"So will I satisfy My wrath on you." (Ezekiel 16:42)

We glimpse God's fierce wrath in Jerusalem's destruction in 587 BC. But chiefly, we see it on the cross. Ezekiel warns us not to spurn Jesus' atonement, lest we risk suffering God's wrath eternally in hell.

Some people, thinking "I've already been through hell," believe God should reward their sufferings. What is the proper way to think of our sufferings, since only Jesus' suffering and death can atone for our sins?

The LORD's Everlasting Covenant (16:59–63)

God promises to punish His Bride through the destruction of Jerusalem. But He will remember His covenant with Israel and restore them. He Himself will atone for Israel through Jesus' life, death, and resurrection.

Parable of Two Eagles and a Vine (17:1–24)

King Jehoiachin has been taken into captivity; King Zedekiah has broken his oath to the Babylonian king and will be defeated and taken captive. Yet God will raise up the promised Messiah from David's descendants.

The Soul Who Sins Shall Die (18:1–32)

WAYPOINT

What does this text show us?
The exiles accuse God of punishing them for their fathers' sins. God says they will each stand before Him and be judged for their own sin unless they repent and believe. Yet God asserts that His desire is to forgive and save, not to kill.

What does this text reveal about God's plan of salvation?
God does not delight in anyone's death but rather desires that we repent and are saved for Jesus' sake. Those who reject Jesus will be judged and condemned by God. But those who believe in Christ will inherit eternal life.

What does this text uncover about our identity and calling as God's people today?
Each of us sinners deserves eternal death and punishment for our sin. When we repent and trust in Jesus, we are forgiven and made righteous. In gratitude, we share that good news with others so God may save them too.

Why do you think the exiles blamed their fathers for their exile?

How can God say the soul who sins will die when Jesus died for your sins and mine?

Why is it so easy to blame others for our sins as these exiles were doing?

A Lament for the Princes of Israel (19:1–14)

Ezekiel portrays Judah's final three kings first as young lions and then as stems of a vine in a vineyard. Because each ruler abused his power, they will be trapped and imprisoned like lions and uprooted and burned like a vine.

VISUALIZE

Israel's Continuing Rebellion (20:1–32)

Certain elders among the exiles come to Ezekiel for a third time to inquire of the Lord through him. But since they worship the gods of the Babylonians, God refuses to listen to their inquiry or answer it.

The LORD Will Restore Israel (20:33–49)

WAYPOINT

What does this text show us?
God will disperse the unrepentant Judeans throughout the Babylonian Empire and restore a faithful, believing remnant to the Promised Land as His covenant people. They will be ashamed of their former idolatry and offer right sacrifices.

What does this text reveal about God's plan of salvation?
God's wrath is stirred by humanity's sinfulness, but in mercy, God sent His Son, Jesus, to bear those sins upon the cross and suffer the punishment we all deserve. For Jesus' sake, God offers forgiveness and salvation to all people.

What does this text uncover about our identity and calling as God's people today?
God is faithful and merciful. He daily forgives us for Jesus' sake, and when Christ returns, He will forever remove our sinful natures and make us pure and holy, giving us eternal life in His glorious presence.

The idea of passing under the shepherd's rod (v. 37) can be frightening when we think of Judgment Day. How would you comfort someone who is fearful of Christ's judgment?

How is it comforting to know that God controls even the actions of unbelieving rulers to accomplish His good purposes for His church?

What experiences in your life would you describe as God's chastening rod turning you away from sinful temptations that would endanger your faith and salvation?

The LORD Has Drawn His Sword (21:1–32)

The king of Babylon will come up to besiege Jerusalem. The prince of Israel, Zedekiah, will be deposed and imprisoned, and Jerusalem will be left a ruin.

PICTURE OF THE SAVIOR

"Until He comes, the one to whom judgment belongs." (Ezekiel 21:27)

In the middle of Ezekiel's prophecy, he gave a fleeting messianic prophecy: After Zedekiah, no descendant of David would again rule as king in Judah until Christ came and said, "The kingdom of heaven is at hand" (Matthew 4:17).

Israel's Shedding of Blood (22:1–31)

The name *Jerusalem* means "city of peace," but the city is filled with bloodshed, idolatry, violence, injustice, and the mistreatment of sojourners, orphans, and widows.

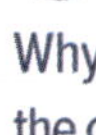

Why is the silversmith smelting the ore such a powerful metaphor for God driving away our sinful impurity? What are some of the fiery trials God has used to purify you (see 1 Peter 4:12)?

SET THE SCENE

Silver Smelting

Smelting silver in Bible times required careful watching. First, the ore was heated in a furnace to remove sulfur elements. Next, the furnace was heated to just the right temperature to remove impurities without destroying the silver.

Oholah and Oholibah (23:1–49)

Ezekiel portrays Israel and Judah as two sisters God married. Both whored after other gods. God gave up Oholah (Israel) to the Assyrians. Now, he will surrender Oholibah (Judah) to the Babylonians.

CLEAR THE CONFUSION

What do *Oholah* and *Oholibah* mean?

Oholah means "her tent." It refers to the two golden calf idols Jeroboam I built to keep his subjects from worshiping at the temple in Jerusalem. *Oholibah* means "my tent is in her," which refers to the Lord's temple in Jerusalem.

The Siege of Jerusalem (24:1–14)

When Nebuchadnezzar's siege of Jerusalem begins, Ezekiel compares the city to a pot filled with meat, set on a roaring fire. Despite the intense pressure God asserts on Jerusalem, the people refuse to repent.

It is easy to think of prophets as bold, faithful servants who experienced no emotions. Clearly this was a heartbreaking experience for Ezekiel, but God used it to increase the impact of his ministry to his fellow exiles. When has God worked dramatic good out of great loss in your life?

Ezekiel's Wife Dies (24:15–27)

In the morning, Ezekiel speaks to the exiles; in the evening, his beloved wife suddenly dies. God charges Ezekiel not to show the normal display of grief and sorrow that was customary in his culture.

Oracles Against Other Nations (25:1–32:32)

Ezekiel pronounces oracles, or prophecies, against seven Gentile nations around Israel. Each of these nations has opposed the coming of God's kingdom through His Son, Jesus Christ.

Prophecy Against Ammon (25:1–7)

The Ammonites despise Israel and had watched the Babylonians defile Yahweh's temple with malicious glee. Because they mocked God and His saving mission, He promises to take them into captivity.

Prophecy Against Moab and Seir (25:8–11)

The people of Moab consider Israel to be no different from every other nation on earth, which is a direct insult to the Lord who dwells with His people. This is similar to people who say Christianity is just another religion.

Few of Israel's neighboring nations sought its destruction as much as the Edomites. In what ways were the Edomites working against their own spiritual welfare and that of their descendants?

Prophecy Against Edom (25:12–14)

The Edomites are hostile to Israel and Judah all through the Old Testament. Not only did they celebrate Jerusalem's destruction with malicious glee but they helped divide the spoils with Babylon.

Prophecy Against Philistia (25:15–17)

The Philistines and Israel were at war during the later period of the judges throughout the reigns of Saul and David. God charges them with "never-ending enmity" (v. 15) against Israel.

Prophecy Against Tyre (26:1–21)

Tyre rejoices over Jerusalem's destruction, because with their major trade competitor gone, Tyre expects its trade networks to increase. It gloats over the destruction of Jerusalem for its own selfish gain.

A Lament for Tyre (27:1–36)

Ezekiel compares the island kingdom to a majestic trading ship skillfully built with the best materials, finest decoration, and experienced sailors and marines to guard it; yet it is lost at sea with all hands.

Prophecy Against the Prince of Tyre (28:1–10)

God charges Tyre's king with excessive pride for claiming to be an exceedingly wise god who has made himself wealthy and invulnerable to attack. God will send the might of Babylon against him.

 CLEAR THE CONFUSION

Is the Daniel of verse 3 the prophet who wrote the book of Daniel?

Yes. Daniel was exiled to Babylon in 605 BC, six years before Ezekiel. Two or three years later, Daniel was promoted in the empire, becoming well known for his wisdom throughout that part of the world (see Daniel 2).

In this lament, look for parallels with Satan's fall, as well as with Adam and Eve. What parallels do you see?

A Lament over the King of Tyre (28:11–19)

Despite the wonderful gifts with which God has endowed Tyre's king, he defiles them through unscrupulous trading practices and selfish pride.

Prophecy Against Sidon (28:20–24)

Sidon, who was a sister city of Tyre, treated Israel with contempt. God promises to punish Sidon so they will acknowledge that He is God.

Israel Gathered in Security (28:25–26)

God will execute judgments on Israel's neighbors who treat them with contempt. Israel will know He is Yahweh, their God, the only true God.

Prophecy Against Egypt (29:1–21)

Pharaoh has led his army out against Babylon, forcing Nebuchadnezzar to temporarily lift Jerusalem's siege. This interference with God's plan to punish Jerusalem was one reason for this prophecy.

Babylon's attack on Egypt and the destruction of Egypt's idols are like a replay of the ten plagues from Exodus. What are some ways God breaks our reliance on our idols of wealth, success, accomplishments, and the like?

A Lament for Egypt (30:1–19)

God will send Babylon to devastate the land of Egypt. All idols will be destroyed and Egypt will know the Lord is God. These false gods have kept Egypt from fearing the Lord and finding salvation in His grace.

Egypt Shall Fall to Babylon (30:20–26)

God describes Pharaoh as a swordsman with a broken arm. God "broke" his arm at the battle at Carchemish, but instead of humbling himself, Pharaoh had lured Judah to rebel against Babylon. Now he must perish.

Pharaoh to Be Slain (31:1–18)

Assyria had been a powerful empire that had risen high above all other nations. In its pride and arrogance, it was suddenly cut down and cast to the grave. Soon the same will happen to proud Pharaoh.

A Lament over Pharaoh and Egypt (32:1–32)

Pharaoh thinks he is an intimidating young lion, but God mocks him as a crocodile confined to its own narrow channel. Ezekiel describes Pharaoh and his armies descending to join the dead.

Oracles and Visions of Israel's Restoration (33:1–48:35)

Ezekiel's final section shifts to sweet Gospel. Ezekiel shares the glorious promise that God will return the exiles to Jerusalem, restore them as His people, and send the Messiah to restore His people and His creation.

Describe a time when you received devastating news that left you fearful and feeling hopeless. Why is it important to step back and look at God's epic plan of salvation and the life of the world to come when Jesus returns, as we do in weekly worship?

Ezekiel Is Israel's Watchman (33:1–9)

God again calls Ezekiel to be Israel's watchman (see also 3:16–21). Though the remaining prophecies will be predominantly Gospel promises, the Law must still be proclaimed so sinners will repent and receive God's grace.

Why Will You Die, Israel? (33:10–20)

God reveals that He takes no pleasure in the death of the wicked but delights when sinners turn to Him in repentance and trust Him to make them righteous through faith in the coming Savior.

Jerusalem Struck Down (33:21–33)

A survivor from Jerusalem reports to Ezekiel that the city has been conquered and struck down. Ezekiel now preaches God's Word to the captive survivors of Jerusalem as well as to his fellow exiles.

Prophecy Against the Shepherds of Israel (34:1–10)

The shepherds of Israel are the political and religious leaders who have failed to care for God's people. The people have wandered around with no true shepherd. Now the sheep are scattered in exile.

The Lord GOD Will Seek Them Out (34:11–24)

God Himself promises to come and seek out the lost sheep and gather them together in good pastureland, where He will feed them with bread from heaven and they will be satisfied.

The LORD's Covenant of Peace (34:25–31)

The Lord promises a covenant of peace with the people of Israel. He will give them abundant food, keep them safe from all enemies, and protect them from being enslaved or suffering the reproach of the nations.

?

As we struggle through trials, temptations, and opposition from Satan, the world, and our sinful nature, what encouragement do you find knowing that God knows and is already restraining and opposing our spiritual enemies?

Prophecy Against Mount Seir (35:1–15)

Edom's sin is its perpetual enmity against Israel. Since their hatred and covetous desire for Israel's land stand in the way of God's plan to restore Israel and return the exiles, He foretells their destruction.

Prophecy to the Mountains of Israel (36:1–15)

God rejects Edom's assertion that it will possess the land of Israel, and He promises the people of Israel will soon come back and possess the land as their inheritance again.

The LORD's Concern for His Holy Name (36:16–21)

Israel has profaned God's name by bloodshed and idolatry. When He punishes them with exile, the Gentiles believe their gods are stronger. God promises to vindicate His name when He restores Israel to their land.

I Will Put My Spirit Within You (36:22–38)

God reminds Judah that all the good He will do for them is not because of what they have done, how sincerely they have repented, or all they have suffered. He will put His Spirit in them and return them to their land.

CLEAR THE CONFUSION

What is meant by the men of Israel being like the flock for sacrifices during Jerusalem's appointed feasts (vv. 37–38)?

During the great festivals (Passover, Pentecost, Tabernacles), the hills around Jerusalem were covered with sacrificial animals. Ezekiel prophesied that the hills of Israel, now bare and desolate, would be resettled and filled with people.

The Valley of Dry Bones (37:1–14)

What thoughts might have occurred to Ezekiel if this was the battlefield where Judah's forces were defeated by Babylon?

How does this resurrection sequence show the role of the Holy Spirit when Christ returns to raise the dead on the Last Day?

How does this vision give us a glimpse into what will happen when Christ returns?

WAYPOINT

What does this text show us?

When Ezekiel prophesies in a valley full of dry bones, the bones return to life to form a large army. God explains that these bones are the exiles' hopes. But God will raise them from captivity and return them to their land.

What does this text reveal about God's plan of salvation?

Judah's exile in Babylon seems like the end of God's promise of salvation, but it is a mere detour. In His time, God will return them from exile to rebuild the temple and await the coming Savior, Jesus Christ.

What does this text uncover about our identity and calling as God's people today?

When Jesus returns on the Last Day, He will give a command and raise us and all the dead to stand before Him in judgment. Believers will live with Him in a new paradise forever, while unbelievers will be cast into hell forever.

CLEAR THE CONFUSION

What is the significance of these dry bones belonging to an exceedingly large army?

These were like the exiles in Babylon. They were powerless to defend their homeland or their families or to raise themselves in battle again. But God will raise the exiles and return them home, as will He raise Jesus from the dead.

I Will Be Their God, They Shall Be My People (37:15–28)

Ezekiel takes two sticks, one for Judah and one for Israel, and joins them as one stick. God will gather them from all the tribes and unite them again as one kingdom under one king, His servant David.

How discouraged are you by the divisions in your congregation or by the divisions in the Christian Church? What comfort does it bring to know Christ will bring perfect unity when He returns at His second advent?

PICTURE OF THE SAVIOR

One Nation Under One King (37:22)

This clearly prophesies the reign of Jesus Christ over His Holy Christian Church. This kingdom is made up of not only believing Israelites but also the Gentiles grafted into Israel by faith.

Prophecy Against Gog (38:1–39:24)

Chapters 38 and 39 detail the great, last battle when Christ returns to establish the new heavens and the new earth. Revelation narrates this same last battle in chapter 20 then describes eternity in chapters 21–22.

CLEAR THE CONFUSION

What are Gog and Magog?

A century before Ezekiel, powerful King Gog of Lydia spread terror through military conquests. Since this passage talks about the time of Christ's return, it is best to see Israel as the Christian Church and Gog and Magog as Satan and our enemies.

The LORD Will Restore Israel (39:25–29)

God will call His exiled people back to their land. He will display His glory among them and never hide His face from them again because He will pour out His Spirit on them.

Vision of the New Temple (40:1–4)

Fourteen years after Solomon's temple had been destroyed, Ezekiel receives a vision of a new temple. God takes him to a high mountain in the land of Israel where he sees a structure like a city.

For the exiled Jews, their vision of heaven was being back at the temple in Jerusalem. That is why this vision was so powerful. What do you visualize when you think of heaven? Where are God the Father and Jesus in your visualization?

VISUALIZE

Ezekiel's Vision of the Temple's Outer and Inner Courts

God gave Ezekiel a vision of a new temple that would never actually be built. As the priestly prophet described each detail, the exiles who yearned to stand in God's presence in the temple hung on his every word.

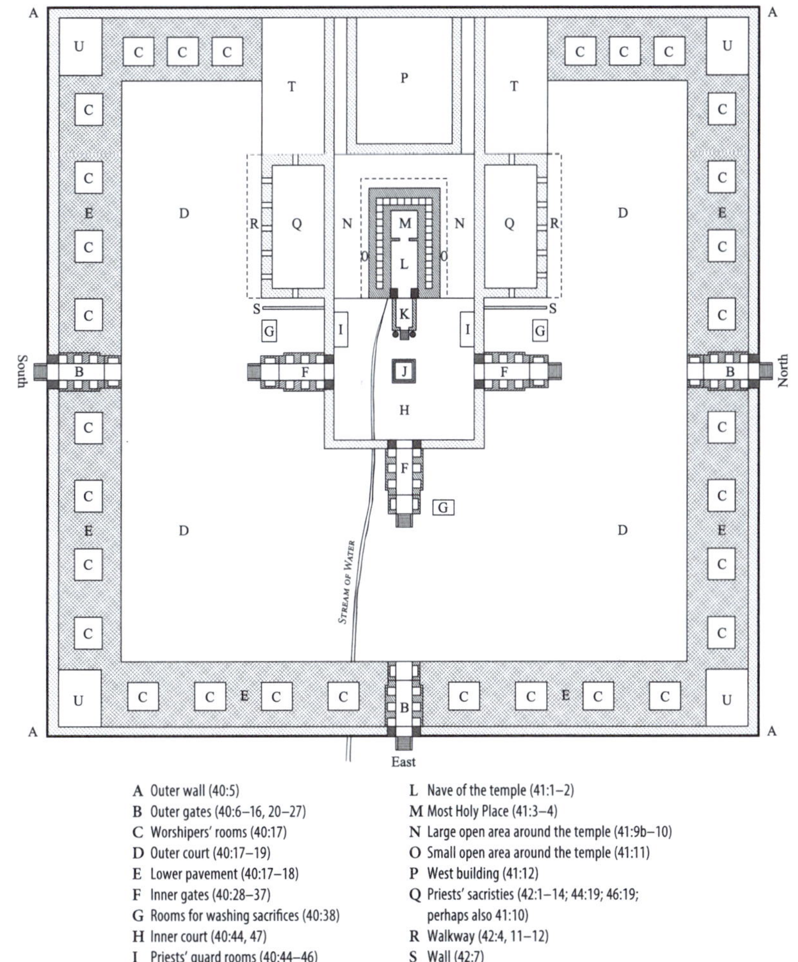

The East Gate to the Outer Court (40:5–16)

Ezekiel is led to the wall surrounding the temple complex. He climbs a set of stairs and passes through the east gate. At the end, the gateway opens into an expansive courtyard, the outer court of the temple.

The Outer Court (40:17–19)

Ezekiel enters a courtyard with thirty chambers in the outer walls. In Solomon's temple, worshipers ate sacrificial meals in these rooms. Ezekiel follows his guide along this outer wall toward the north gate.

Approaching God's presence in Ezekiel's temple involved ascending higher and higher on three sets of stairs. How does this ascent carry the idea of approaching God's throne and leaving earthly things behind? Does the architecture of your church's worship space incorporate raised platforms to remind you of this heavenly ascent?

The North Gate (40:20–23)

Ezekiel sees that the north gate is identical to the east gate through which he first entered. Across the outer court from this north gate is an internal north gate, which leads from the outer court to the inner court.

The South Gate (40:24–27)

Ezekiel is led along the wall to the south side, where he finds an identical outer gate with identical features and measurements. God's temple has a wonderful order, symmetry, and majesty.

The Inner Court (40:28–43)

Ezekiel is led toward the inner court where he first glimpses the new temple. Each inner gate is identical to the three outer gateways, except instead of seven steps leading up to the gate, these gates have eight steps.

Chambers for the Priests (40:44–47)

In the inner court, right outside the temple, Ezekiel sees the altar on which sacrifices are burned, as well as a room for the priests who officiate at the altar and another for those who officiate inside the temple.

Ezekiel must have felt wonder and excitement standing in front of the temple doors. How can we recapture that wonder when standing in front of our church doors?

The Vestibule of the Temple (40:48–49)

Ezekiel now approaches the front doors of the temple itself. He climbs ten steps, passes between two pillars, and arrives at an enclosed space right in front of the temple doors.

VISUALIZE

Ezekiel's Vision: The Temple and the Altar

The temple shown to Ezekiel in chapters 41–43

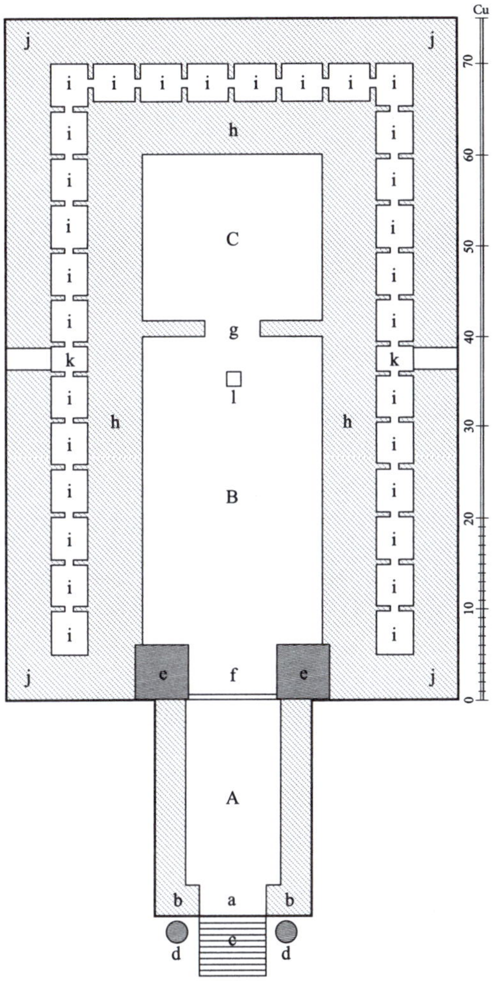

A Vestibule (40:48–49)
B Nave (41:1–2)
C Most Holy Place (41:3–4)
a Doorway of the vestibule (40:48)
b Doorposts of the vestibule (40:48–49)
c Steps (40:49)
d Pillars (40:49)
e Doorposts of the nave (41:1)
f Entrance of the nave (41:2)
g Entrance of the Most Holy Place (41:3)
h Wall of the temple (41:5)
i Side rooms (41:5–7)
j Outer wall of side rooms (41:9)
k Entrance of the side rooms
l Table (41:22)

The Inner Temple (41:1–26)

Ezekiel is led into the temple. Like the tabernacle and Solomon's temple, it consists of two rooms, the Holy Place and the Most Holy Place. A wooden altar or table stands in front of the Most Holy Place.

The Temple's Chambers (42:1–20)

Ezekiel is led back out of the temple. He sees the chambers in which the priests eat the holiest offerings and change their vestments so the holy clothing is never worn into the outer court among God's people.

The Glory of the LORD Fills the Temple (43:1–12)

How does this movement of God through the east gate reverse His movement when forsaking the temple earlier in Ezekiel?

What do you picture in your mind when you think of what it means to dwell in the presence of God in heaven?

What are some things we do in worship that remind you of Christ's presence among us (e.g., bowing toward the altar, crossing yourself)?

WAYPOINT

What does this text show us?
Ezekiel sees the glory of the Lord coming from the east, His glory illuminating the earth beneath. The glory of the Lord passes through the east gate. From the temple, God tells Ezekiel He will dwell in this place with His people forever.

What does this text reveal about God's plan of salvation?
God has taken away our sins and made us holy to enter His presence for Jesus' sake. On the Last Day, Christ will judge the living and the dead, cast all evildoers into hell, renew the creation, and dwell among us forever.

What does this text uncover about our identity and calling as God's people today?
On Judgment Day, Christ will return to restore His shattered creation and dwell with us forever. He has sent us to our fellow exiles to teach them that He has taken away our sins so we can dwell with Him forevermore.

The Altar (43:13–27)

God prescribes seven days to consecrate the altar. This reflects creation week and prefigures Holy Week. On the eighth day, Easter Sunday, He rose to life to serve us forever as Prophet, Priest, and King.

VISUALIZE

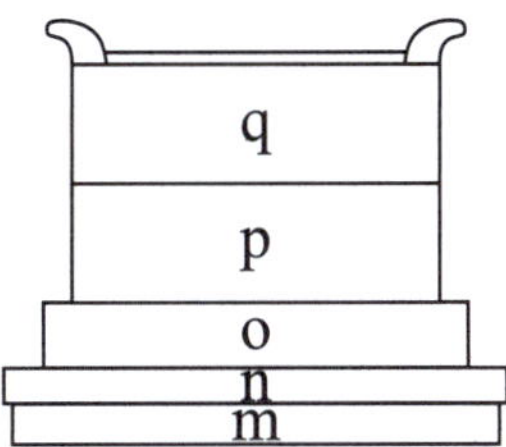

q Hearth (43:15–16)
p Larger, upper ledge (43:14; perhaps also 43:17)
o Smaller, lower ledge (43:14; perhaps also 43:17)
n Ridge (43:13; perhaps also 43:17)
m Gutter (43:13–14; perhaps also 43:17)

PICTURE OF THE SAVIOR

The Altar

The altar in Ezekiel's vision (vv. 13–17) is raised up nearly twenty feet above ground, making it a focal point that draws all eyes to it. In this way, it foreshadows Jesus lifted up on the altar of the cross.

The Gate for the Prince (44:1–14)

Since the glory of the Lord has entered the temple complex through the east gate, no one else is to ever enter by that gate. The closed gate is a promise that God will never again abandon His people.

Rules for Levitical Priests (44:15–31)

The Levitical priests who were descended from Zadok are to distinguish the clean from the unclean and teach Israel to do the same. The priests receive no land inheritance because God is their inheritance.

In what ways are the responsibilities of pastors today similar to those of the Levitical priests in Ezekiel's vision, especially regarding teaching people to distinguish between the clean and the unclean?

The Holy District (45:1–6)

VISUALIZE

The Holy District

The holy district consists of three parallel strips. The northern strip is for the priests and includes the temple complex. The center is for the other priests and the Levites. The lower strip includes the city of Jerusalem.

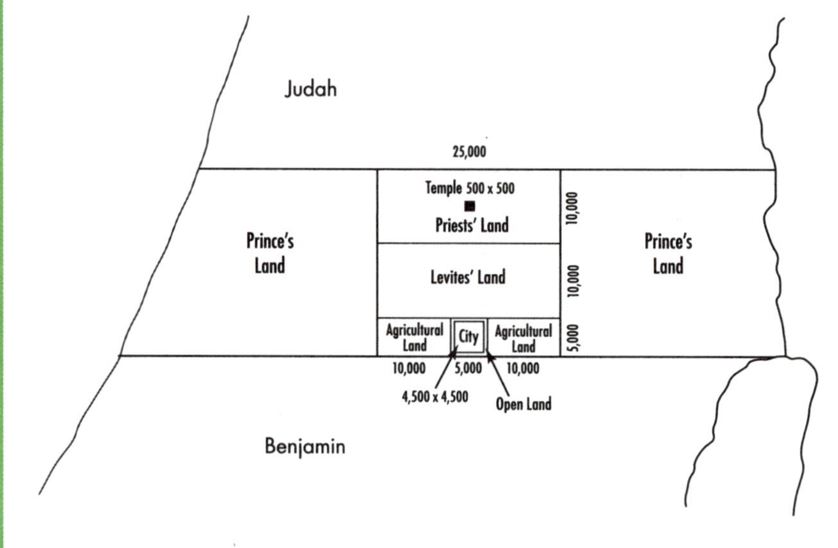

The Portion for the Prince (45:7–25)

Two portions of land alongside the holy district are set aside for the prince. He will supervise worship and provide the sacrificial animals for the various festivals as well as the Sabbath and new moon observances.

The Prince and the Feasts (46:1–18)

VISUALIZE

Unlike the Davidic kings with Solomon's temple, the prince is to supervise worship and provide the sacrifices. How does this point forward to Jesus and His great sacrifice on the cross?

Boiling Places for Offerings (46:19–24)

Ezekiel sees two sets of kitchens. Those in the inner court prepare the priests' sacrifices and those in the outer court prepare the meals for God's people, so that all may eat in the presence of the Lord.

What does the phrase "river of life" mean to you?

Water Flowing from the Temple (47:1–12)

Ezekiel's vision closes with the curse on creation being removed and the heavens and earth restored to the former perfection. Water flows from the temple door. The further it goes, the deeper it becomes.

LINK BETWEEN THE TESTAMENTS

The River of Life (Ezekiel 47:1–12 → Revelation 22:1–2)

Both Ezekiel and John describe this same river. In Ezekiel, it flows from God's presence in the temple. In Revelation, the river flows from God's throne. In Revelation, it nourishes the tree of life, which grows on both banks of the river.

Division of the Land (47:13–48:29)

The land is divided between the twelve tribes. Notice the special provision allowing Gentiles to inherit land as if they were native-born children of Israel.

To the exiles, a walled city was the picture of peace and security. To know that God was there at all times increased the joy, comfort, and security. What image or place captures this same sense for you?

The Gates of the City (48:30–35)

Ezekiel closes with the twelve gates of the city of Jerusalem. It will forever be called "The Lord Is There"—a beautiful picture of our eternal life in the presence of God, the Father, Son, and Holy Spirit.

DANIEL

Welcome to Daniel

The book of Daniel looks at the challenges Daniel and his three fellow Judeans experienced in the pagan governments of the Babylonian and Persian Empires. Daniel illustrates how God is with His people, controlling events and even pagan leaders according to His holy will. As you read Daniel, consider that your God still controls your world—His creation—no matter what society's leaders and influencers may say.

Which parts of Daniel are familiar to you? What are you hoping to learn as you study this book?

Daniel at a Glance

- **Start:** Daniel is exiled from Jerusalem and trained to serve in the Babylonian court.
- **End:** The Son of God describes events in the New Testament era leading to His return to raise the dead and judge the world.
- **Theme:** The Most High God controls all things that happen among humans, and He always works for the benefit of His kingdom and His people.
- **Author and Date:** The prophet Daniel most likely wrote in the early years of Cyrus, king of Persia, after the fall of Babylon. He looks back over his experiences in Babylon and the early years of Persia between 605 and 536 BC.
- **Places Visited:** Judah, Babylon, Media, and Persia
- **Journey Time:** The twelve chapters of Daniel can be read in approximately an hour and a half.
- **Outline:**
  - Judeans Steadfast in Practicing Their Faith (1:1–21)
  - Nebuchadnezzar's Dream (2:1–49)
  - God's Faithful Servants Rescued from Death (3:1–30)
  - Nebuchadnezzar Judged for His Arrogance Against God (4:1–37)
  - Belshazzar Judged for His Arrogance Against God (5:1–31)
  - God's Faithful Servant Rescued from Death (6:1–28)
  - Daniel's Visions (7:1–12:13)

Five Top Sights and Spectacles of Daniel

Daniel Interprets Nebuchadnezzar's Dream (2:31–45) Hear the gasps of wonder as Daniel tells the king what his dream means.

The Fiery Furnace (3:8–30) Feel the blast of heat as three Judeans are cast into the overheated furnace.

The Handwriting on the Wall (5:5–30) Watch in horror as an eerie hand appears and writes on a palace wall.

The Lions' Den (6:1–28) Hold your breath as an anxious king calls out to see if Daniel is still alive.

The Preincarnate Christ Speaks with Daniel (10:1–12:4) Tremble in wonder as Daniel listens to God's Son.

Seeing Jesus in Daniel

Jesus' eternal kingdom is mentioned in several chapters. The preincarnate Christ rescues Daniel's three companions in the fiery furnace, and He appears to Daniel and speaks throughout the last three chapters. Perhaps most significantly, Daniel learns "an anointed one shall be cut off and have nothing" (9:26), foreshadowing Jesus' crucifixion. The result of Jesus' substitutionary death is "to finish the transgression, to put an end to sin, and to atone for iniquity" (9:24).

Judeans Steadfast in Practicing Their Faith (1:1–21)

Through four young Judeans taken captive and pressed into service in the Babylonian government, God will protect His people and teach great rulers of the world that He is sovereign over every nation on earth.

Daniel Taken to Babylon (1:1–7)

Babylonian King Nebuchadnezzar takes vessels from the temple and exiles some Judeans. From these, he selects youth to be educated, assimilated into Babylonian culture, and prepared for service in the royal court.

Daniel's Faithfulness (1:8–21)

Daniel and his companions obey God's dietary laws despite pressure. After their training, Nebuchadnezzar finds Daniel and his companions much better than all the other youth and even his own court magicians.

When Daniel's request to eat vegetables was first denied, how did he use respect and tact to be able to keep obeying God? How can you do the same at work or school?

Nebuchadnezzar's Dream (2:1–49)

The king is troubled by a dream and becomes furious when he can find no one to interpret it.

Nebuchadnezzar's Dream (2:1–16)

During Daniel's training period, the king has a troubling dream. He commands his dream experts to reveal both his dream and its interpretation. When they can't, he orders all the wise men in the empire executed.

CLEAR THE CONFUSION

Why did Nebuchadnezzar insist the dream experts reveal the dream itself as well as its interpretation?

He knew his experts could concoct a favorable interpretation to flatter him and make him think all would be well. But if they had a real connection with the gods, the gods would reveal the dream and he could trust their interpretation.

God Reveals Nebuchadnezzar's Dream (2:17–30)

Daniel and his three companions pray for God's mercy. In a night vision, God reveals the mystery. When Daniel is brought to Nebuchadnezzar, he tells the king, "There is a God in heaven who reveals mysteries" (v. 28).

How is Daniel interpreting Nebuchadnezzar's dream similar to Joseph interpreting Pharaoh's dream so many centuries before (Genesis 41)? How do these passages assure us God knows and controls our future?

Daniel Interprets the Dream (2:31–45)

Babylon is the first of four mighty kingdoms that will span the time between the close of the Old Testament and the coming of the Christ. God will send the Messiah and His kingdom will endure forever.

PICTURE OF THE SAVIOR

The Rock That Becomes a Mountain

Jesus is the rock not cut by human hands. He was conceived by the power of the Holy Spirit, not by any man. The rock growing into a mountain pictures the growth of the Christian Church throughout the New Testament era.

God arranged Daniel's promotion to benefit all His people throughout the Babylonian Empire. How are faithful Christian leaders in politics, business, and the church a benefit to all people?

Daniel Is Promoted (2:46–49)

Nebuchadnezzar praises Daniel's God as "God of gods and Lord of kings" (v. 47). He promotes Daniel over the province of Babylon and makes him chief prefect over the wise men.

God's Faithful Servants Rescued from Death (3:1–30)

While Daniel is in the royal court, Shadrach, Meshach, and Abednego govern affairs in the Babylon province. When Nebuchadnezzar demands all people worship his image, the three take a stand to obey the Lord.

Nebuchadnezzar's Golden Image (3:1–7)

The king orders all his officials to attend the dedication and to fall down and worship the image when the music plays. Anyone refusing the order will be thrown into a burning fiery furnace.

How do Daniel's friends model the Fourth Commandment—that we honor and obey the authorities over us unless they demand that we disobey God?

The Fiery Furnace (3:8–30)

Shadrach, Meshach, and Abednego disobey the king's command. Nebuchadnezzar gives them a warning and another chance, but they refuse to obey him, putting their trust in the Lord instead.

VISUALIZE

CLEAR THE CONFUSION

Who was the fourth man in the fire?

Some think this was an angel, but Nebuchadnezzar said, "The appearance of the fourth is like a son of the gods" (v. 25). Though it could have been an angel, it seems more fitting for this to have been the preincarnate Christ.

Nebuchadnezzar Judged for His Arrogance Against God (4:1–37)

God humbles Nebuchadnezzar's arrogance and conceit to make him a more just and merciful ruler and to move him to confess his sins and receive God's salvation through faith.

Think about a time when you saw a leader acting arrogantly and oppressing others. What happened, and was there any consequence?

Nebuchadnezzar Praises God (4:1–3)

In an open letter to his people, Nebuchadnezzar describes the miraculous way God humbled him. He acknowledges that God's kingdom is everlasting and His dominion endures forever.

Nebuchadnezzar's Second Dream (4:4–18)

Nebuchadnezzar relates feeling prosperous and secure until he has a second troubling dream. After his dream experts fail to interpret it, he summons Daniel.

Daniel Interprets the Second Dream (4:19–27)

The king will be driven from society and live in the wild until he acknowledges God. Daniel urges him to repent and show mercy. We see God actively ruling the nations for the benefit of His people.

CLEAR THE CONFUSION

Why was Daniel dismayed when he heard the dream?

Daniel had to confront the sinful lifestyle of this powerful king. Notice how Daniel said he wished it would happen to the king's enemies. Daniel did everything he could so the king would hear God's word with an open heart.

Nebuchadnezzar's Humiliation (4:28–33)

After twelve months, Nebuchadnezzar still feels secure in his sin. While he is boasting about how he built his kingdom, a voice from heaven announces that judgment has come.

Nebuchadnezzar Restored (4:34–37)

At the end of the prescribed time, Nebuchadnezzar looks up to heaven and his sanity and kingdom are restored. He closes his letter by praising God, who is able to humble the proud and truly rules all kingdoms.

Belshazzar Judged for His Arrogance Against God (5:1–31)

Daniel now jumps ahead to the last Babylonian king, Belshazzar. Like Nebuchadnezzar, Belshazzar acts arrogantly against the Lord; unlike Nebuchadnezzar, he will not humble himself before Daniel's God.

We see many leaders here and around the world who defy God and flaunt their arrogance. What comfort do you receive from reading this account of God's writing on the wall?

SET THE SCENE

Babylon's Last Night

King Belshazzar held a drunken feast as the armies of Persia were at Babylon's walls. Why feast instead of oversee the city's defense? This is not even the worst decision Belshazzar would make on this, his final night as ruler of Babylon.

The Handwriting on the Wall (5:1–12)

Belshazzar commands the vessels of the Lord's temple be brought for his guests to drink from as they toast their false gods. Immediately, a human hand appears, to the king's great terror.

Belshazzar spent his last night in drunken feasting rather than humble repentance. How would you try to reach someone like him who lives for today and gives no thought to his or her eternal future?

Daniel Interprets the Handwriting (5:13–31)

Daniel reminds Belshazzar how Nebuchadnezzar humbled himself before the Lord. He confronts Belshazzar for mocking God by drinking from His sacred vessels instead of humbling himself.

God's Faithful Servant Rescued from Death (6:1–28)

Daniel's three companions had refused to bow down to an image. Now, Daniel refuses to stop praying to his God. Notice carefully the differences between Nebuchadnezzar and Darius.

How did Daniel's enemies take advantage of Darius's pride?

Daniel and the Lions' Den (6:1–28)

Darius the Mede plans to appoint Daniel over the whole Persian Empire. In jealousy, the other officials conceive a plot to destroy Daniel. Anyone who prays to any deity besides the king must be thrown into a den of lions.

VISUALIZE

CLEAR THE CONFUSION

Why did Daniel pray toward Jerusalem when he knew the temple had been destroyed?

When Solomon dedicated the temple, he asked God to answer prayers that His exiled people prayed toward Jerusalem (1 Kings 8:27–53). Daniel trusted God's promise to Solomon that He would answer those prayers (1 Kings 9:3).

PICTURE OF THE SAVIOR

Parallels Between Daniel's Experience and Jesus' Passion

- Malicious accusers sought the death of each of them.
- Unruly crowds brought each before a pagan ruler with accusations of violating the law.
- The ruler considered the man before him innocent and sought to set him free until pressured by the crowd to execute him.
- A rock was placed over the opening of the pit and of the tomb, both of which were sealed with a royal seal.
- At dawn, the king hurried to the pit; the women rushed to Jesus' tomb.
- When the stone was rolled away, each emerged from the tomb alive.

Daniel's Visions (7:1–12:13)

Four visions show Daniel how God will take the dominion from the nations and give it to the Messiah, Jesus Christ. These visions prepare the returned exiles for days of opposition before Jesus' first coming.

Daniel's Vision of the Four Beasts (7:1–8)

Daniel receives this first vision during the reign of Belshazzar, the last coregent to rule before Babylon fell to Darius. This vision consists of four beasts rising out of the great sea.

The returned exiles living in Judea during the intertestamental time faced great upheaval and uncertainty at the hands of these four empires. Daniel's visions remind them God is in control throughout. How can these visions bring us comfort when we experience political upheaval in our world?

CLEAR THE CONFUSION

What were the four beasts?

The first beast was the Babylonian Empire. The second was the Persian Empire. The third was the Greek Empire of Alexander the Great. The fourth beast was the Roman Empire.

The Ancient of Days Reigns (7:9–12)

Daniel sees thrones set up and the eternal God, the Ancient of Days, sitting in judgment at court.

What do you think when you consider Jesus sitting at the right hand of God the Father, governing all things in heaven and on earth for the benefit of His Bride, the church?

The Son of Man Is Given Dominion (7:13–14)

Daniel sees one "like a son of man" who comes on the clouds and is presented to the Ancient of Days. God the Father gives Him dominion, glory, and a kingdom to rule over all peoples, nations, and languages.

PICTURE OF THE SAVIOR

The Son of Man Coming on the Clouds

Jesus refers to Daniel 7:13–14 as He foretells His second coming: "And they will see the Son of Man coming on the clouds of heaven with power and great glory" (Matthew 24:30).

Daniel's Vision Interpreted (7:15–28)

Deeply troubled by the vision, Daniel asks what it means. Daniel further asks about the fourth kingdom and especially the little horn that warred against the kingdom of God.

What kinds of insecurity do you think the Jews faced with the rise and fall of so many empires? How well do you handle changes in your workplace or community?

Daniel's Vision of the Ram and the Goat (8:1–14)

At the canal in the Persian capital of Susa, Daniel sees a mighty ram with two horns and a goat with one large horn charging from the west. This foreshows the fall of the Persian Empire and the rise of the Greek Empire.

Hellenization: Trying to Turn Israel Greek

Between the testaments, the Greek Empire pushed to spread the Greek language and culture throughout their empire. God's people struggled to resist this push to adopt the Greek culture and religions.

Greek became the universal language throughout the Roman Empire that replaced Greece. The New Testament was written in common Greek and spread quickly through the Roman Empire.

The Greeks worked hard to make all the peoples they conquered adopt their Greek culture, a process called hellenization. Where do you see our culture working hard to make the church and other institutions adopt its values and viewpoints?

The Interpretation of the Vision (8:15–27)

Daniel seeks to understand the vision and God sends the angel Gabriel to explain the details, even naming the two nations—Persia and Greece—which helps confirm our interpretation from previous chapters.

LINK BETWEEN THE TESTAMENTS

Gabriel (Daniel 8–9 → Luke 1)

The angel Gabriel makes his first appearance in the Bible in the book of Daniel. Hundreds of years later, Gabriel appears to the priest Zechariah to announce the birth of a son, John the Baptist. Six months later, Gabriel visits a virgin of Nazareth to announce she will conceive and bear God's Son.

Daniel did not base his prayer request on his obedience or Israel's suffering but on God's gracious promises. How can you bring God's promises into your prayers when you encounter difficult situations, fears, and doubts?

Daniel's Prayer for His People (9:1–19)

In the first year of the Persian Empire, Daniel confesses that God was just and right to punish Israel, but now he asks the Lord to return the exiles so they can restore the city and rebuild the temple.

Gabriel Brings an Answer (9:20–23)

As soon as Daniel begins praying, God sends Gabriel with His answer. Gabriel comes swiftly at the time of evening sacrifice. He assures Daniel that he is forgiven and greatly loved.

The Seventy Weeks (9:24–27)

WAYPOINT

What does this text show us?

A decree will start the return of the exiles, the rebuilding of the temple, and the restoring of divine service. Some time later, the Messiah will come. He will be cut off (executed by crucifixion). The temple and city will be destroyed.

What does this text reveal about God's plan of salvation?

Jesus, the Messiah, will be cut off in order "to finish the transgression, to put an end to sin, and to atone for iniquity, to bring in everlasting righteousness" (v. 24). Jesus' sacrifice will win salvation for all.

What does this text uncover about our identity and calling as God's people today?

The Judeans rejected and killed God's Messiah. The resulting destruction of the temple ended temple sacrifice. We live in Christ's everlasting righteousness now and for all eternity.

How do you expect Daniel responded when he learned the Messiah would be executed?

Jesus was "cut off"—that is, executed, or crucified. How did His suffering and death atone for iniquity?

How might this vision's description of the Messiah being cut off have been hard for Daniel and his fellow exiles to receive? Why is Jesus' death still a stumbling block to people today?

Daniel's Terrifying Vision of a Man (10:1–21)

After Daniel fasts and mourns for three weeks, a man clothed in linen speaks to him. Daniel is terrified and can only stand and listen to the revelation after the man touches and strengthens him three times.

PICTURE OF THE SAVIOR

Daniel and Jesus Both Strengthened by an Angel (Daniel 10:10–19; Luke 22:43)

Just as Daniel needed strength to see the vision and understand its interpretation, Jesus needed strength to continue to pray under the weight of His intense grief. The angel did not remove Jesus' agony but gave Him the strength to bear that agony and wrestle in prayer until He was at peace.

What comfort do you derive from knowing God sent angels to strengthen His people and even His own Son in the past?

The Kings of the South and the North (11:1–45)

Two Greek kingdoms vie for control of Canaan. A perverse ruler of the north will persecute the Jewish people and attempt to stop worship in the new temple. This ruler, Antiochus IV, prefigures the antichrist.

LINK BETWEEN THE TESTAMENTS

The Abomination That Makes Desolate (Daniel 11:31 → Matthew 24:15)

Daniel describes a violation of the temple that caused great devastation. Jesus warns His disciples to flee Jerusalem when they see the abomination that causes desolation—Roman legions marching toward the temple.

How does this vision given to Daniel make you long for Christ's return so many centuries and millennia later?

The Time of the End (12:1–13)

Christ foretells the resurrection of all, the judgment of all, and the glorious future awaiting the saints. He promises Daniel will rest in death, then stand in his allotted place at the resurrection.

CLEAR THE CONFUSION

Who are those who "sleep in the dust" (v. 2)?

This refers to the dead of all ages who will be raised to life and judgment when Christ returns. The Bible uses the analogy of sleep to emphasize God's power over death (see Psalm 17:15; Isaiah 26:19; Mark 5:39; 1 Thessalonians 4:13–16).

LINK BETWEEN THE TESTAMENTS

Unprecedented Times of Distress and Trouble (Daniel 12:1 → Matthew 24:29–30)

On Tuesday of Holy Week, Jesus predicted to His disciples this same period of intense distress and trouble as Daniel had—both when the Roman troops attacked the temple in AD 70 and shortly before His return on Judgment Day.

HOSEA

Welcome to Hosea

Hosea is the first of the twelve prophets known as the minor prophets. They are not less important than Isaiah, Jeremiah, Ezekiel, or Daniel; their books are simply shorter. These books together took up one scroll, while each major prophet took up a scroll by itself.

When Hosea wrote, Israel had been divided for nearly two centuries. The Northern Kingdom had enjoyed prosperity, expanded borders, and economic security but was now drifting away from the Lord into idolatry. God sends Hosea to turn this Northern Kingdom back to Him.

Hosea uses the metaphor of marriage to expose Israel's unfaithfulness and to highlight God's love. See your God's love in His willingness to confront His people in their sin so He can call them back to Himself.

In what ways is our relationship with God like a marriage? How do faithfulness, forgiveness, and trust impact both of these relationships?

Hosea at a Glance

- **Start:** Hosea begins during the righteous reign of Judah's King Uzziah and the evil reign of Israel's King Jeroboam II. Hosea is set just after Jonah prophesied in Nineveh and Amos in Israel.
- **End:** Hosea ends during the righteous reign of King Hezekiah over Judah. At this same time, Isaiah prophesied in Judah.
- **Theme:** Although we are unfaithful to God like Hosea's wife is, God remains faithful to us and redeems us from our life of sin.
- **Author and Date:** The prophet Hosea wrote during the reigns of Uzziah, Jotham, Ahaz, and Hezekiah, kings of Judah. His prophecies were compiled after Israel was taken into Assyrian captivity.
- **Places Visited:** Israel, Ephraim, Beth-aven, Judah, and Assyria
- **Journey Time:** The fourteen chapters of Hosea can be read in about half an hour.
- **Outline:**
  - Hosea's Personal Issues as Prophecies (1:1–3:5)
  - Various Oracles (4:1–14:9)

Five Top Sights and Spectacles of Hosea

Living Prophecy (1:2–2:1) Learn from Hosea as God uses his wife and children to teach Israel through enacted prophecy.

Hosea Redeems His Wife (3:1–5) Watch Hosea redeem his unfaithful wife back from her lover and renew his commitment to her.

Whirlwind of Idolatry (8:7–10) Discover the futility of idolatry as Hosea prophesies that Israel will reap desolation and exile.

Steadfast Love for Israel (11:1–9) Behold God the Father as He shows mercy to Israel despite their idolatry and unfaithfulness.

Seeking Reconciliation (14:1–7) Hear Hosea's plea for Israel to return to the Lord for forgiveness, health, and security.

Seeing Jesus in Hosea

Just as Hosea married an unfaithful woman, Jesus pursued His Bride, the church, and bought us back from sin and unfaithfulness with His blood. Although our sin leads us to walk away from God, Jesus saves us.

Hosea's Personal Issues as Prophecies (1:1–3:5)

Hosea's devotion to his unfaithful wife helps us better understand how our sins offend our God and highlight His boundless mercy and grace.

Introduction (1:1)

Hosea denotes the time when he prophesied. He prophesied for approximately forty years throughout the reigns of five kings.

CLEAR THE CONFUSION

Why did Hosea tell us the kings of both Israel and Judah?

Though God sent Hosea to the Northern Kingdom of Israel, he listed all four Judean kings and omitted numerous Israelite kings to illustrate Israel's long history of unfaithfulness to God.

Hosea's Wife and Children (1:2–11)

God calls Hosea to marry an unfaithful woman. As Gomer bears children, God names each child in a way that warns Israel of impending disaster but also shows His steadfast love for the children of Israel.

WAYPOINT

What does this text show us?
Hosea's personal life vividly shows God's pain at Israel's unfaithfulness. As Gomer bears children to Hosea and to her lover, the Lord proclaims the impending consequences of Israel's idolatry.

What does this text reveal about God's plan of salvation?
Through Hosea, God not only exposes Israel's unfaithfulness but also demonstrates His faithfulness by renewing His promise to reclaim Israel as His people and to look on them in mercy.

What does this text uncover about our identity and calling as God's people today?
God uses human language to communicate His will through the Bible. In the Sacraments, God's Word unites His promises with tangible elements of water, bread, and wine to vividly show us His everlasting love.

Take a moment and really think about what Hosea did for Gomer. Would you be willing to marry someone knowing that he or she will be unfaithful to you?

How has God used the people in your life to teach you more about Him?

How do the Sacraments help you understand God's will more clearly?

Read the First Commandment and its explanation in Luther's Small Catechism. How have you been unfaithful to God by breaking this commandment?

Israel's Unfaithfulness Punished (2:1–13)

God personifies Israel as a wife and mother. Hosea asks for the children of Israel to plead for the nation to repent. God sends punishments to Israel in order to curb their path so they will repent and return to Him.

The LORD's Mercy on Israel (2:14–23)

God reveals His steadfast love and desire for Israel, promising that He will woo and betroth Himself to Israel once more, offering forgiveness for Israel's infidelity and renewing His covenant with them.

CLEAR THE CONFUSION

My Husband or My Baal?

The Hebrew word for *Baal* means "lord" or "master," a pet name Israelite women used for their husbands. Through this clever wordplay, God emphasized Israel's proper relationship with Him as husband and wife.

Take a moment to reflect on the price Jesus paid for your redemption. Does it make you ashamed that your sins cost His life? Or does it make you appreciate God's love more that He loved you enough to pay that price?

Hosea Redeems His Wife (3:1–5)

After Gomer abandons Hosea for her lover, God sends him to redeem her from her infidelity. Hosea buys Gomer back from her lover, restoring his marriage and encouraging her not to turn away in infidelity again.

VISUALIZE

PICTURE OF THE SAVIOR

The Price of Redemption

Through Hosea's enacted prophecy, God illuminated our relationship with Him. Although we turned away to other gods, He sent His only Son to redeem us from our sin. Jesus gave His life to pay the price for our idolatry.

Various Oracles (4:1–14:9)

The remaining chapters of Hosea turn to various oracles in which God warns of destruction and calls Israel to repent and be saved.

The LORD Accuses Israel (4:1–19)

God accuses Israel for their many sins. He narrows His charges against Israel's priests who have led the people in idolatry. God expresses His desire for Judah to learn from Israel and turn from idolatry.

SET THE SCENE

Cult Prostitution

Worship of fertility gods such as Baal often involved the use of cult prostitution, where worshipers would have illicit sexual relationships with prostitutes at the deity's temple in order to bring rain and fertility to the land.

Punishment Coming for Israel and Judah (5:1–15)

God proclaims His judgment against Israel, especially the royal family for their bloody history and role in leading Israel astray. God declares He will depart from Israel and they will be carried off into exile.

When have you reaped the consequences of your own sin? Do you normally "get away with" your sins?

Israel and Judah Are Unrepentant (6:1–7:16)

When Israel suffers military defeat, they only turn to God half-heartedly, seeking His aid without recognizing their own sin. God allows Assyria to keep assailing them because of their deceitful repentance.

Israel Will Reap the Whirlwind (8:1–14)

God uses a farming metaphor: Israel has sown seeds of idolatry, building idols in Samaria and establishing numerous sites for idol worship. In the end, they will reap a harvest of sin, facing the devastating Assyrian exile.

WAYPOINT

What does this text show us?
After the first King Jeroboam had sown the seed of idol worship with his golden calves, Israel waters their sin by continuing in this worship. Hosea prophesies about the day when they must reap the harvest of punishment for their sin.

How did generations of worshiping the golden calves make idol worship difficult for the Israelites to escape?

On the cross, how did Jesus reap the destruction for the sin we sowed?

The Bible makes it clear that death and hell are the eternal punishments for our sin. What are some of the consequences of our sins in this life?

What does this text reveal about God's plan of salvation?
All who sow sin will always reap destruction, whether they experience it in this life or in eternity. But Jesus Christ sowed righteousness by His life, death, and resurrection. Through Spirit-given faith, we reap salvation and eternal life.

What does this text uncover about our identity and calling as God's people today?
As we live by faith in God, the Spirit empowers us to sow good works that will produce fruit in our lives. While life apart from God bears a harvest of destruction, life in Christ bears a harvest of eternal life.

The LORD Will Punish Israel (9:1–10:15)

God describes the coming desolation of Israel. Some will flee to Egypt and die there, while others will be carried away to Assyria. Israel's children will die, and the kingdom of Israel will be thoroughly destroyed.

PICTURE OF THE SAVIOR

The Hated Prophet

Israel mocked Hosea and rejected his message, trying to drive him mad and setting traps for him. Jesus also faced rejection throughout His earthly ministry. The Jewish authorities ignored Jesus' calls to repentance. The Pharisees and Sadducees set logical traps for Him. Together they plotted to crucify Him.

The LORD's Love for Israel (11:1–12:1)

God expresses His steadfast love for Israel through the metaphor of father and son, calling for Israel to return and avoid complete destruction.

The LORD's Indictment of Israel and Judah (12:2–14)

What was the difference between Jacob wrestling with God the night before he met Esau and the way the Northern Kingdom was wrestling against God?

God points to Jacob's life to give Israel an example of how to properly strive with God against sin and evil. He condemns Israel for hiding behind wealth to deny their sins and fighting against Him in unrepentant sin.

CLEAR THE CONFUSION

What was God's indictment against Judah?

Most of Hosea's prophecies are against Israel, but he occasionally prophesied against Judah's idolatry and oppression of the helpless. God will spare Judah from the Assyrian exile because of King Hezekiah's repentance and prayer.

The LORD's Relentless Judgment on Israel (13:1–16)

God condemns Israel's child sacrifice and their ingratitude for His deliverance. In response, He chooses not to have compassion because of Israel's refusal to repent.

How do you reconcile God's boundless love in Christ with Judgment Day and the sentence of hell for unbelievers? What do you have trouble wrapping your mind around?

PICTURE OF THE SAVIOR

Shall I Redeem My People?

In Hosea, God decided not to have mercy on Israel because of their horrific, unrepentant sin. Ultimately, God had mercy on us by pouring His wrath upon His own Son on the cross, punishing Him for our sins. Through Christ's sacrifice, God has mercy on us and will raise us on the Last Day to eternal life with Him.

A Plea to Return to the LORD (14:1–9)

WAYPOINT

What does this text show us?
Because God is the faithful husband of Israel, His desire is for her repentance and He waits earnestly to defend her, be her sole provider, and restore His relationship with her.

What does this text reveal about God's plan of salvation?
God desires for all to be saved—to turn to Him for forgiveness, life, and salvation. He desires to be our sole God, providing for our every need during our earthly lives as we trust fully in Him.

What does this text uncover about our identity and calling as God's people today?
As God's people, we lean on His mercy and supply for our every need. When we fall into sin, we can rely on Hosea's message that God will heal our apostasy and love us freely, offering us the forgiveness Christ won for us on the cross.

How do God's words give us courage to repent and lay our sin and guilt before Him?

Has there ever been a time when someone forgave you even after you broke his or her trust repeatedly?

Throughout Hosea, we have seen God repeatedly call Israel to repentance. How does God continue calling us even when we ignore Him?

JOEL

Welcome to Joel

Joel is a gentle, soft-spoken prophet. He does not lash out with scathing Law, as we will see in later prophets, but emphasizes God's unfailing love for His people. Joel prophesies an agricultural disaster—armies of locusts tearing through Judah's farmlands, leaving nothing but stubble behind.

Joel demonstrates both the heights of God's wrath and the depths of His mercy. Christ took our punishment upon Himself as He died on the cross. In faith, we turn to Him and call upon His name for deliverance from sin, death, and the devil. As you read Joel, think of your Savior, Jesus, quietly and gently calling you from sin to eternal life.

How do natural disasters affect your faith? Do they pull you away from God or draw you to Him?

Joel at a Glance

- **Start:** Joel begins with a swarm of locusts devastating Judah's crops and threatening hunger and starvation.
- **End:** Joel ends with the coming of the Holy Spirit at Pentecost, the New Testament era, and Christ's return to judge the world.
- **Theme:** Our sin brings devastation, but God will have mercy on all who repent and will send His life-giving Spirit to all nations.
- **Author and Date:** We don't know exactly when the prophet Joel wrote this book.
- **Places Visited:** Judah, Greece, Mount Zion, the barren fields, the temple, and the nations surrounding Judah
- **Journey Time:** The three chapters of Joel can be read in about twelve minutes.
- **Outline:**
    - Catastrophes, Current and Coming (1:1–2:17)
    - The Lord's Response (2:18–3:21)

Five Top Sights and Spectacles of Joel

A Great Drought in Judah (1:15–20) Weep with Judah as they watch crops wither in the fields from a devastating drought.

The Invasion of Locusts (2:1–11) Cower before an invading army of locusts, which brings judgment for Israel's unrepentant sins.

Rend Your Hearts and Not Your Garments (2:12–17) Hear the Lord's call to return to Him with our whole hearts.

God's Spirit for All People (2:28–32) Take comfort as God sends the Holy Spirit and invites us to call upon Him in times of trouble.

Reckonings for the Nations (3:9–16) Gird yourself for war as God promises vengeance on the nations that oppressed Judah.

When you go to church next Sunday, keep your bulletin and look through it again later. How often did you call upon the name of Jesus during the service?

Seeing Jesus in Joel

As God speaks of the outpouring of His Holy Spirit, He promises that "everyone who calls on the name of the LORD shall be saved" (2:32). By His death on the cross, Jesus won deliverance for all believers.

Catastrophes, Current and Coming (1:1–2:17)

Joel opens his book with a call to repentance so Judah will be spared an agricultural disaster more devastating than any they can remember.

INTRODUCTION (1:1)

Joel presents his prophetic credentials: The word of the Lord came to him with a message to declare to the people of Judah.

AN INVASION OF LOCUSTS (1:2–12)

Joel recounts the unprecedented invasion of locusts that ate all of Judah's crops, and he calls the people of Judah to lament with him because of the devastation it has brought upon their agriculture.

Locusts

The region around Israel frequently dealt with locust swarms, in which vast numbers of locusts flew together and devoured all plant life within the area before leaving to find new plants to feast on. Joel references four kinds of locusts, which likely refer to various stages in the life cycle of a desert locust.

A Call to Repentance (1:13–20)

Joel turns to the priesthood to lead Judah's repentance by wearing sackcloth and fasting. He then prophesies a great drought that will cause Judah's livestock to suffer.

During Lent, many Christians fast from meat on Fridays or cut out something else from their life to help them focus on God. What can you fast from to help you focus on your faith?

Fasting in the Bible

Fasting and sackcloth both emphasized humility and repentance before God by abandoning the comforts of food and soft clothing. When mourning, however, the lack of comfort represented the wearer's bereavement.

The Day of the LORD (2:1–11)

VISUALIZE

WAYPOINT

What does this text show us?

Joel warns about the coming day of the Lord, prophesying another horrendous swarm of locusts. These locusts represent the swarm of nations and armies God will lead against Judah to devastate Jerusalem and plunder the land.

How is a locust invasion similar to a military invasion?

What does this text reveal about God's plan of salvation?
To those who live in sin and ignore God's commandments, the day of the Lord will bring judgment. God desires for us to repent and turn to Him, relying on His steadfast love as He relents from the disaster awaiting us.

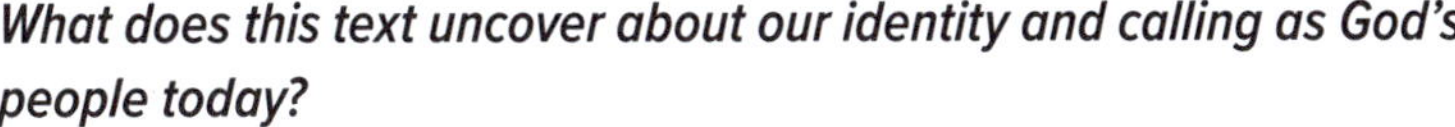

What does this text uncover about our identity and calling as God's people today?
Like the people of Judah, we are called to repent of our sin, knowing that Christ has borne our punishment on the cross so that we may look forward to the day of the Lord as a day of hope rather than a day of punishment.

How does God demonstrate His power through His mighty deeds on the day of the Lord?

Why do you look forward to the day of the Lord?

SET THE SCENE

The Day of the Lord

The prophets frequently spoke of the day of the Lord as the Last Day, when God will bring this world to an end. These prophecies promise restoration and vindication to God's righteous people but threaten punishment for the wicked.

LINK BETWEEN THE TESTAMENTS

Horses on the Day of the Lord (Joel 2:4–11 → Revelation 9:7–11)

In his prophecy of the Last Day, Joel saw the invading enemy as horses charging into Jerusalem to desolate the city. In Revelation, demonic forces swarm the earth like locusts. Like those in Joel, these locusts look similar to horses, and the sound is like horse-drawn chariots rushing into battle.

Return to the LORD (2:12–17)

God calls Judah to repent in their hearts, not just in the outward signs of a fast. Joel commands the priesthood to lead another fast, motivated by true repentance rather than empty religious performance.

When you worship, how do you keep yourself from simply going through the motions or treating it like an empty ritual?

LINK BETWEEN THE TESTAMENTS

False Repentance (Joel 2:12–17 → Matthew 23:25–26)

God calls Judah to rend not just their garments but also their hearts. Jesus criticizes the Pharisees' self-indulgent desire to impress people by their words and deeds—thus telling the Pharisees that they must repent in their hearts.

The Lord's Response (2:18–3:21)

Joel describes all the Lord will do if Judah repents. He describes events of Jesus' first coming and the Holy Spirit being poured out on the church.

The LORD Had Pity (2:18–27)

Seeing Judah's repentance, God has mercy and removes the threat of northern invaders, promising to restore Judah's agriculture through abundant rains and demonstrating His steadfast love to His chosen nation.

 **CLEAR THE CONFUSION**

Who is the northerner God is removing (v. 20)?

"The northerner" could refer to the Assyrian armies, who would conquer Israel and ravage the land of Judah until God struck them down, or it could point forward to Babylon, which would conquer Judah and lead them into captivity.

Unlike in the Old Testament when the Holy Spirit was only given to specific individuals at specific times, God gives the Holy Spirit to all Christians in Baptism. How does this affect our relationship with God?

The LORD Will Pour Out His Spirit (2:28–32)

Beyond the physical restoration of Judah through abundant harvests, God also promises spiritual blessings as He pours out His Spirit on all people and delivers all who call on Him.

 **WAYPOINT**

What does this text show us?
God's abundant grace overflows, giving His people more than deliverance from the invading enemy. He also promises to send spiritual gifts through the Holy Spirit, and He promises salvation through faith in Christ.

What does this text reveal about God's plan of salvation?
God sent His Son as a human to bear the punishment for our sins and win our salvation by His death and resurrection. He poured out His Spirit to create saving faith that receives that salvation.

What does this text uncover about our identity and calling as God's people today?
We can be certain of our identity as God's people because through Baptism He grants His Holy Spirit to every Christian, adopting each one of us into His family and giving us assurance of our salvation in Christ.

What emotions would this prophecy be likely to stir in a Judean who heard it?

What spiritual gifts does God give us because He has delivered us from sin, death, and the devil?

How does Baptism transform you and give you a new identity as a Christian?

LINK BETWEEN THE TESTAMENTS

God's Spirit (Joel 2:28–32 → Acts 2:16–21)

This prophecy points forward to Pentecost, when Jesus poured out the Holy Spirit upon the apostles and they spoke in tongues to Jews gathered in Jerusalem from all across the ancient world.

The LORD Judges the Nations (3:1–16)

God broadens His scope beyond Judah, promising judgment on the surrounding nations who oppressed them. He calls the nations to prepare for war as He avenges Judah's suffering.

The Glorious Future of Judah (3:17–21)

WAYPOINT

What does this text show us?
God shows His faithfulness to His chosen people, vindicating Judah as He brings judgment to Judah's enemies and oppressors. He promises to restore Judah to glory, elevating His people above all other nations.

What does this text reveal about God's plan of salvation?
Through this passage, we experience God's faithfulness and zeal for His people. As He extended His promises of salvation to Israel and Judah, we can be sure that He will extend these promises to us and restore us to glory on the Last Day.

What does this text uncover about our identity and calling as God's people today?
In our Baptism, God has claimed us as His own and has adopted us into His family. This passage reminds us that He will vindicate us on the Last Day, restore us to glory, and bring judgment on those who have oppressed us.

How does God undo the works of Satan and restore the glory of His children?

God designed Old Testament Israel to be a mission nation to the Gentiles. How did their idolatry interfere with that mission?

What physical blessings has God given you in addition to His spiritual blessings?

AMOS

Welcome to Amos

Amos is the third of the twelve minor prophets. He confronts a people secure in their sin. The Lord is a just God whose holiness demands sin be punished. He shows us the fires of hell we deserve in order to lead us to repent and turn to Christ Jesus, who suffered in our place on the cross.

Amos is a shepherd and fig tree farmer in Judah when God calls him to prophesy to the Northern Kingdom during the reign of King Jeroboam II (see 2 Kings 14:23–29). Israel is enjoying a time of economic security but keeps drifting further and further from God. As you read Amos, consider if you are drifting and, if so, ask Christ to pull you back.

?

Amos preaches to a people caught up in success and prosperity. Which earthly things most threaten to ensnare you?

Amos at a Glance

- **Start:** The book starts with condemnation of the Gentile nations, which spirals in on Israel.
- **End:** The book ends with Amos conveying God's promise to send the Messiah to rescue those who repent and believe Him.
- **Theme:** The people of Israel turn to idols and oppress the helpless and vulnerable. The people will go into exile and only a remnant will repent and be saved.
- **Author and Date:** Amos recites the calamities and warnings the Lord provides to him in visions. The book was written during the reign of Jeroboam II, placing it around 760–750 BC.
- **Places Visited:** Israel, Judah, Gaza, Damascus, Tyre, Edom, Ammon, and Moab
- **Journey Time:** The nine chapters of Amos can be read in just under thirty minutes.
- **Outline:**
    - Proclamation of Judgment (1:1–2:16)
    - Israel's Sins and Refusal to Repent (3:1–6:14)
    - Visions (7:1–9:15)

Five Top Sights and Spectacles of Amos

God's Punishment Enacted on the Nations (1:2–2:16) Hear the extent of God's anger against the sins of Israel and their neighbors.

Pagan Temples at Bethel Destroyed (3:13–15) Listen to Amos's poetic depiction of God visiting His wrath on the false temple at Bethel.

God Proclaims Plagues for Israel (4:6–11) Witness God sending plagues upon Israel to bring them to repentance and faith.

God Sends Warning Visions of Locusts and Fire (7:1–9) Feel Amos's fear and compassion when the Lord shows him devastating visions.

Amos Glimpses the Coming of the Messiah (9:11–15) Listen to Amos describe the coming of Jesus Christ and the New Testament church.

Seeing Jesus in Amos

Amos warns of impending judgment for those who abused their power in Israel. But in the final part of the book, God promises to raise up the Messiah, Jesus Christ, from the fallen line of David.

Proclamation of Judgment (1:1–2:16)

Amos begins with eight judgments against surrounding nations then finally for Judah and Israel.

Introduction (1:1)

Amos provides the setting for his ministry. He is a shepherd in Judah, called to prophesy in Israel during the prosperous reign of Jeroboam II.

SET THE SCENE

The Earthquake

Amos prophesied two years before "the earthquake" (v. 1). It must have been extremely damaging given that even after the Babylonian captivity Zechariah refers to it (Zechariah 14:5).

Judgment on Israel's Neighbors (1:2–2:3)

WAYPOINT

What does this text show us?
Amos declares the Lord's displeasure with the nations around Israel and lists their specific sins against God and His people. Amos implies that God is like a lion roaring from the temple in Jerusalem, warning of coming punishment.

What does this text reveal about God's plan of salvation?
The nations around Israel have forsaken the Lord God and have been guilty of atrocious sins. God exposes the sin of fallen humanity to lead us to repent and find forgiveness in Jesus, who suffered the punishment for all our sins.

What does this text uncover about our identity and calling as God's people today?
We are all sinful by nature and need God to call out our sins and lead us to repentance. When He gives us pardon, forgiveness, and peace in the Gospel of Jesus, we can share that Law and Gospel with others.

What are the war crimes these nations have committed?

How does God reassure you of His mercy despite your sin?

Why is it sometimes difficult to accept God's mercy shown to others?

CLEAR THE CONFUSION

What does the formula used throughout this passage, "For three transgressions of . . . , and for four, I will not revoke the punishment," indicate?

Only one sin is mentioned for the first six Gentile nations, but each is a vicious war crime. The formula of three, then four shows the escalating wickedness that God will punish. Each time this formula is repeated, the intensity grows.

Judgment on Judah (2:4–5)

Judah is the seventh on Amos's list of nations who have sinned against God. They rejected His law, broke His statutes, and turned to idols. God will send fire upon the people of Judah.

Satan tempts us, like the people of Judah, to abuse God's grace in Christ by indulging our sins and excusing ourselves. What sin do you find yourself underestimating in your life?

Judgment on Israel (2:6–16)

God reminds Israel how He delivered them from slavery in Egypt, yet they sell their own poor into slavery now. When God sends prophets to confront their sin, the Israelites silence them. (We will see a priest at Bethel try to silence Amos in chapter 7.)

VISUALIZE

Israel's Sins and Refusal to Repent (3:1–6:14)

God now turns to address the sin and unrepentance of all His people, both Israel and Judah.

Israel's Guilt and Punishment (3:1–4:5)

Amos attacks Judah's and Israel's royalty, merchants, and rich upper class who oppress the poor. God shows how He will wrench away their prosperity and comfort and inflict hardship instead.

CLEAR THE CONFUSION

What were the winter and summer houses (3:15)?

Israel's climate was hot in the summer and cold in the winter. Wealthy Israelites oppressed the poor, widows, and fatherless to accumulate the wealth to build these seasonal mansions.

Israel Has Not Returned to the LORD (4:6–13)

Amos shares a list of judgments similar to the plagues God sent on Egypt when Pharaoh refused His command to free Israel (Exodus 7–12). Since Israel refuses to repent, God Himself will appear to judge Israel.

Seek the LORD and Live (5:1–17)

Amos takes up a lament. When the people of Israel ask who has died, whom he is lamenting, Amos says he is lamenting them. Unless they repent, the Lord will bring death and destruction upon them all.

Looking back over your past, what priorities do you consider a senseless waste? What current priorities might you consider a waste when you are on your deathbed? How can such reflection lead to repenting and amending our lives?

CLEAR THE CONFUSION

What is a lamentation (v. 1)?

A lamentation is a rhythmic dirge, a song of mourning often associated with a tragic, senseless death. This was not a song praising the deceased but grieving the disgraceful way they died.

Let Justice Roll Down (5:18–27)

The unfaithful Israelites think their sacrifices satisfy God. Amos warns them the day of the Lord will be darkness and not light; they will be hunted and destroyed by God.

CLEAR THE CONFUSION

What does the metaphor of fleeing from wild animals mean (v. 19)?

This verse speaks of the impossibility of escaping God's punishment. Not a single Israelite will be able to escape the coming invasion. The moment he thinks he has escaped, he will run right into something else that will kill him.

Woe to Those at Ease in Zion (6:1–14)

Those who feel secure in their wealth and greatness and who partake in sinful pleasure and lives of ease will be the first to go into exile. God's wrath will be so vehement the survivors will fear to utter His name.

CLEAR THE CONFUSION

What does Amos mean when he talks about "beds of ivory," singing "idle songs," and drinking "wine in bowls" (vv. 4–6)?

Instead of seeing that the poor, widows, and orphans were provided for, the wealthy Israelites lived opulent lives of wine, women, and song. It is reminiscent of Jesus' teaching about the rich man and Lazarus in Luke 16:19–31.

When have you found yourself most tempted to be self-reliant and forsake God? Which experiences in your life have driven you to recognize your need, repent, and return to God?

Visions (7:1–9:15)

God presents a series of visions to Amos to preach to His people.

Warning Visions (7:1–9)

God shows Amos two devastating visions. When Amos cries out, God relents of both. In a third vision, God promises not to avert His judgment any longer.

CLEAR THE CONFUSION

What is a plumb line (v. 7)?

A plumb line is a string with a weight on the end. As the builder holds the string, gravity pulls the weight straight down. From ancient times to today, builders have used plumb lines to ensure that walls and supports are straight.

Amos Accused (7:10–17)

Amaziah, the priest of Bethel, tries to intimidate Amos and force him to flee. Amos asserts that the Lord sent him to prophesy. Amaziah will die in exile in a foreign, ungodly nation.

Think of a time someone tried to intimidate you into silence. What tools does God give us to overcome such intimidation?

The Coming Day of Bitter Mourning (8:1–14)

In a fourth vision, Amos attacks the deceitful business practices Israel's merchants use to exploit the poor. He warns that famine and drought will strike and even the vigorous young men and women will die.

What ethical standards are important in your line of work? Why is honesty important for society in general?

PICTURE OF THE SAVIOR

On That Day

God foretells many of the events of Good Friday in this passage:

I will make the sun go down at noon and darken the earth in broad daylight. (Amos 8:9)	→	It was now about the sixth hour [noon], and there was darkness over the whole land until the ninth hour, while the sun's light failed. (Luke 23:44–45)
I will turn your feasts into mourning. (Amos 8:10)	→	And all the crowds that had assembled for this spectacle, when they saw what had taken place, returned home beating their breasts. (Luke 23:48)
I will make it like the mourning for an only son. (Amos 8:10)	→	When the centurion and those who were with him, keeping watch over Jesus, saw the earthquake and what took place [when He died], they were filled with awe and said, "Truly this was the Son of God!" (Matthew 27:54)

How can recalling the events of our Lord's suffering and death on Good Friday lead us to repentance and faith?

The Destruction of Israel (9:1–10)

Amos recounts the fifth and final vision from the Lord. God stands beside the altar in Bethel, calling for the temple to collapse on the people of Israel.

The Restoration of Israel (9:11–15)

How does the text show the lowly state of David's royal line in the days before Jesus' birth?

What encouragement do you get from God's patience and faithfulness despite the sinful disobedience of David's sons?

What difference does it make to know that Jesus did all that was required to give you eternal life?

What does this text show us?
God promises to restore the house of David, and the Messiah's kingdom will comprise believers from all nations. They will enjoy prosperity and righteousness.

What does this text reveal about God's plan of salvation?
God promises to raise up one of David's sons as the promised Messiah. In the fullness of time, God sent His Son, born of the virgin Mary.

What does this text uncover about our identity and calling as God's people today?
Jesus Christ has won our salvation by His perfect life, innocent suffering and death, and glorious resurrection from the dead. Through faith in Christ, our sins are forgiven and we will live with Him in paradise forever.

OBADIAH

Welcome to Obadiah

Obadiah is the fourth of the twelve minor prophets and the shortest book in the Old Testament. Obadiah condemns Edom, a nation that victimized God's people in their greatest hour of need. He reminds Israel that God has not forgotten their mistreatment. He promises the restoration of Israel, the return from exile, and the coming of God's messianic kingdom. As you read Obadiah, consider times you have felt completely helpless and overpowered. Jesus Christ is your strong defender.

What do you remember about the relationship between Jacob, whose descendants were the Israelites, and Esau, whose descendants were the Edomites?

Obadiah at a Glance

- **Start:** The book starts with Obadiah condemning Edom for their wickedness toward Israel.
- **End:** The book ends with Obadiah proclaiming the coming kingdom of God, where God's people will hold the territory of every nation and every nation will be a part of the kingdom.
- **Theme:** The Edomites sin against God through their jealousy, hatred, and arrogance toward the Israelites, especially when God sends foreign powers to punish His wayward nation.
- **Author and Date:** The author is the prophet Obadiah. Not much is known about him. He likely wrote in the time between Jerusalem's fall in 587 BC and Edom's fall in 553 BC.
- **Places Visited:** Israel and Edom
- **Journey Time:** Obadiah's twenty-one verses can be read in about five minutes.
- **Outline:**
  - The First Proclamation Against Edom: Humiliation (vv. 1–4)
  - The Second Proclamation Against Edom: Displacement (vv. 5–7)
  - The Third Proclamation Against Edom: Destruction (vv. 8–18)
  - Israel's Restoration and the Kingship of Yahweh (vv. 19–21)

Five Top Sights and Spectacles of Obadiah

God Curses Edom for Her Pride (1–4) Hear God's displeasure at the heartless cruelty of Israel's brother.

God Promises to Decimate the Wisdom of Edom (8–9) Listen to God threatening the destruction of Edom's knowledge and wisdom.

God Threatens All Nations like Edom with His Day of Judgment (15–16) Tremble as you hear God condemn all sinful nations.

Israel Will Be Exalted over Edom and Her Oppressors (17–19) Watch as God holds fast to His promises to restore Israel.

God Promises to Establish His Kingdom on Earth (20–21) Rejoice as God proclaims Himself a refuge for all who trust in Him.

Seeing Jesus in Obadiah

Like the Edomites, Jesus' enemies mocked and ridiculed Him while He suffered on the cross for our sins. Jesus pleaded for their forgiveness and died to reconcile even the violent nations and bring them into His kingdom.

As we await Christ's return, we remember God is patient, giving all people time to hear His Word, repent, and believe in Jesus Christ. How can we guard against stubborn unrepentance at the seeming delay of Jesus' return?

Edom Will Be Humbled (1–9)

Obadiah declares the Lord's wrath on Edom for their actions against the Israelites and because of their arrogance.

CLEAR THE CONFUSION

Why did Edom live "in the clefts of the rock" (v. 3)?

Isaac's son Esau and his descendants, the people of Edom, occupied a rugged, mountainous region that invaders found difficult to attack. This gave Edom a false sense of security and invincibility.

Edom's Violence Against Jacob (10–14)

The Lord is displeased with Edom because they profited off the misfortune that befell Judah. Their gloating and boasting has marked them for a downfall at God's hand.

Men of Edom gloat over the Babylonian destruction of Jerusalem.

The Day of the LORD Is Near (15–18)

The day of Edom's judgment is at hand, but all nations will be encompassed in God's wrath. Edom is a warning for all nations that react with pride, evil, and arrogance while preying on their less fortunate neighbors.

For unbelievers, the day of the Lord will be the day of their death or the day Christ returns to judge the world. How does your Baptism transform the day of the Lord into a day of rejoicing and hope?

When did Edom drink on God's holy mountain (v. 16)?

When Solomon's temple was destroyed, the Edomites stood on the site and drank a cup of triumph to gloat and celebrate. God did not take kindly to that.

The Kingdom of the LORD (19–21)

Obadiah concludes his book with a picture of God's kingdom, which will see the restoration of Israel and all the faithful exiles in His name.

Both Edom and Israel serve as object lessons for us so we will recognize the judgment and suffering that come upon all who are arrogant and indifferent and those who are unfaithful. How does God guard you from these spiritual sins?

CLEAR THE CONFUSION

Where are the Negeb and the Shephelah (v. 19)?

The Negeb is the wilderness area in the south of Judah. The Shephelah is the low foothill area between Philistia on the west and Judah on the east. This passage was a prophecy of the Christian Church growing throughout the world.

JONAH

Welcome to Jonah

Jonah is the fifth of the twelve minor prophets. Jonah disobeys God's command to go to Nineveh, the capital of Assyria. Through a saving miracle, God sets him back on course and ensures that His message for a violent nation unaware of His impending judgment reaches the people of Nineveh. As you read Jonah, compare his reluctance to help the Ninevites with Christ's love for those who sought and took His life.

What parts of Jonah are familiar to you?

Jonah at a Glance

- **Start:** The book begins with God telling Jonah to proclaim Nineveh's destruction to its citizens.
- **End:** The book ends abruptly as Jonah spitefully laments God's mercy in sparing the city of Nineveh, while God questions the justification for Jonah's anger.
- **Theme:** This book demonstrates God's compassion for a world of lost sinners, the Holy Spirit's power to move wicked humans to be contrite and to humble themselves before God, and the Lord's great mercy and forgiveness toward those who repent.
- **Author and Date:** The prophet Jonah wrote this book during the reign of Jeroboam II of Israel. Jonah was a prophet in the Northern Kingdom of Israel (2 Kings 14:25). He most likely wrote this book around 790 BC.
- **Places Visited:** Israel, the Mediterranean Sea, inside a great fish, Nineveh (located on the Tigris River), and Joppa
- **Journey Time:** Jonah's four chapters can be read in eight minutes.
- **Outline:**
  - Jonah Flees the Lord's Calling (1:1–2:10)
  - Jonah Preaches God's Warning and Laments Its Effects (3:1–4:11)

As you read through Jonah, examine the difference between repentance and obstinance. Which characters repent? Which ones don't? Why?

Five Top Sights and Spectacles of Jonah

God Sends a Tempest to Waylay Jonah's Ship (1:4–16) Experience the sailors' fear as they sail into a tempest that threatens their ship.

Jonah in the Fish's Belly (1:17–2:10) Hear Jonah's prayer as God spares his life inside a great fish for three days and three nights.

The People of Nineveh Repent (3:6–10) Watch as an entire city turns from its wickedness to follow God's will.

God Grows a Vine (4:6) Enjoy the refreshing cool as God appoints a vine-like plant to grow quickly and give Jonah shade.

God Sends a Worm (4:7) Smolder under the blazing sun as a worm destroys the plant that had shaded Jonah.

Seeing Jesus in Jonah

In Matthew 12:40, Jesus compared Jonah's three days and nights in a fish to His three-day burial. Whereas Jonah was a reluctant prophet, Jesus loved and willingly preached to the people to whom He was sent.

Jonah Flees the Lord's Calling (1:1–2:10)

Like Jonah, Jesus slept through a storm that nearly sank His ship. Do you tend to worry through the storms of life or rest easy?

Though Jonah disobeys God, the Lord uses the words of the prophet to bring the sailors to faith. How have you seen God's ability to bring good out of your sins or those of others?

When God commands Jonah to preach in Nineveh, the reluctant prophet turns in the opposite direction.

Jonah Flees the Presence of the LORD (1:1–6)

God commands Jonah to preach to the Assyrians in Nineveh. Jonah refuses and flees on a ship for Tarshish. But God appoints a storm to stop the ship and set Jonah back on God's path.

Jonah Is Thrown into the Sea (1:7–16)

The sailors cast lots to learn who has angered the gods. When the lot falls on Jonah, he commands the sailors to throw him into the sea.

A Great Fish Swallows Jonah (1:17)

God sends a great fish to swallow Jonah up and deliver him from death in the waters. He remains in the fish for three days and three nights.

God spared Jonah's life through the great fish. How has God shown you His mercy?

VISUALIZE

CLEAR THE CONFUSION

The Great Fish

The Hebrew language does not distinguish between fish and whales. Regardless of what type of swimming animal God sent, it preserved Jonah's life to carry out the mission God had given him.

Think about a time when you called out to God in prayer. What was the situation? How did God respond?

Jonah's Prayer (2:1–10)

From the stomach of the fish Jonah prays to the Lord, thanking God for not forsaking him despite his disobedience. He vows to fulfill God's will.

LINK BETWEEN THE TESTAMENTS

Jonah's Three Days in the Belly of the Fish → The Sign of Jonah (Jonah 1:17, 2:10 → Matthew 12:38–42; 16:4; Luke 11:29–32)

The Pharisees demanded a miraculous sign from Jesus. He told them that just as Jonah spent three days and nights in the belly of the great fish, so He would spend three days and nights in the belly of the earth, His grave.

Jonah Preaches God's Warning and Laments Its Effects (3:1–4:11)

Jonah is ready to obey when God sends him again, but he is not pleased with the results.

Jonah was reluctant to go to Nineveh. Where is someplace you needed to go but really didn't want to? Why were you reluctant to go there?

Jonah Goes to Nineveh (3:1–5)

At the Lord's command, Jonah goes to Nineveh. He travels one day into the city and then proclaims its destruction in forty days.

SET THE SCENE

Nineveh

Nineveh served as the capital of the Assyrian Empire. The city was located on the banks of the Tigris River in the Euphrates Valley. In addition to enjoying a wealth of agricultural resources, Nineveh lay along major trade routes.

The People of Nineveh Repent (3:6–10)

When Jonah's word reaches the king of Nineveh, he commands his entire city to repent. He orders a fast extending even to the cattle.

The people of Nineveh heeded God's message to repent. When have you been surprised at someone's response to God's message?

Jonah's Anger and the LORD's Compassion (4:1–11)

WAYPOINT

What does this text show us?

When Jonah is outraged by His mercy, God comforts him with a shady plant then lets a worm make it wither. When Jonah complains, God asks if He should not be more concerned about 120,000 human souls than a mere vine.

What does this text reveal about God's plan of salvation?

The Lord loves every person He has created. His Law condemns and His Gospel brings about repentance and faith. We see this action in the Ninevites, who responded to Jonah's warning with repentance, and in His mercy to Jonah.

What does this text uncover about our identity and calling as God's people today?

The Lord promises to give us His Spirit to help us truly love others and to guide us in sharing His Word with those who need to hear the Good News of salvation in Christ.

What prejudgments hinder you from reaching out to others with the love of Christ?

How have you seen God's patience when you have not been as eager to serve as you should be?

How does the success of Jonah's preaching underscore the power of the Holy Spirit working through the Gospel?

MICAH

Welcome to Micah

Micah is the sixth of the twelve minor prophets. Micah warns both Israel and Judah of the impending judgment they are bringing upon themselves through their wayward practices and sin. The book swings between these threats of the Law, visions of God's kingdom to come, and glimpses of the promised messianic King. As you read Micah, consider your sins, which stir God's wrath, and flee to Jesus Christ, who took your sin and willingly suffered in your place.

Many readers are familiar with Micah 5:2, "But you, O Bethlehem Ephrathah," which identifies Jesus' birthplace in Bethlehem. What else would you like to learn about the book of Micah?

Micah at a Glance

- **Start:** Micah begins his prophecies with a poem depicting the execution of God's wrath and judgment on the people of Israel.
- **End:** The book ends with a proclamation of God's love and forgiveness, which contrasts with the doom and despair cast by His wrath.
- **Theme:** Micah strives to turn the Israelites' hearts back to God and give them hope to endure periods of exile and tribulation.
- **Author and Date:** Micah was from a small town in Judah called Moresheth. He prophesied through the reigns of Jotham, Ahaz, and Hezekiah.
- **Places Visited:** Jerusalem, as well as cities in the northern kingdom of Israel
- **Journey Time:** It takes about twenty minutes to read through all seven chapters of Micah.
- **Outline:**
  - Prophecies of Doom Against Various Cities (1:1–3:12)
  - The Coming of God's Salvation and His Rescue (4:1–5:15)
  - Renewed Prophecies of Doom, Ending with Restoration (6:1–7:20)

Five Top Sights and Spectacles of Micah

God's Wrath on His People (1:2–16) See a vision of destruction to be unleashed upon Israel and Judah, including Jerusalem itself.

The Mountain of the Lord (4:1–5) Hear God's kingdom described as a large mountain as God invites Israel to repent.

Jesus' Birth Prophesied (5:1–6) Listen to Micah proclaim that a Savior and King will be born in Bethlehem.

Micah's Sacrifice to the Lord (6:6–8) Follow Micah to learn the depths he is willing to go to appear blameless before the Lord.

God Destroys the Wicked of the World (6:9–16) Marvel at how the Lord renders judgment on those who defy His laws.

Seeing Jesus in Micah

As with the prophet Isaiah, Micah's imagery and poetic prophecies speak of Jesus' coming in the future to establish God's kingdom. Micah details Jesus' birthplace in Bethlehem and His role as Savior and King.

Prophecies of Doom Against Various Cities (1:1–3:12)

Micah opens with prophecies against various cities.

Introduction (1:1)

Micah is a prophet from Moresheth. He prophesies during the reigns of Jotham, Ahaz, and Hezekiah and rebukes Judah and Israel for their sins.

The Coming Destruction (1:2–16)

Micah prophesies the downfall of Samaria and Jerusalem. Their idol worship and immorality are despicable to the Lord, and Micah laments for them. May their judgment be a warning to all nations.

Micah prophesies the coming destruction of Jerusalem. What coming destruction does our world face? What are some of the things in this world that can lead us into a false sense of confidence?

LINK BETWEEN THE TESTAMENTS

The Lord Coming in Judgment → The Final Judgment (Micah 1:3–4 → Matthew 25:31–46)

Micah described God coming down to judge and punish the sins of Samaria and Jerusalem. Jesus described Judgment Day, when He will come down to judge the living and the dead of every nation.

Woe to the Oppressors (2:1–13)

Micah condemns those who oppress the poor and weak. God burns with anger at injustice and wickedness. He will shepherd His people once more and be their King despite their rebelliousness.

PICTURE OF THE SAVIOR

A Shepherd to His Sheep

God's people would be scattered from the Promised Land, but God would gather His people as a shepherd gathers his scattered sheep. Jesus explained that He is our Good Shepherd, who lays down His own life for His sheep (John 10:1–16).

Rulers and Prophets Denounced (3:1–12)

Micah strikes out against the rulers and false prophets who devour their own people. God will ignore their cries during the last judgment.

Why does it make sense that the rulers and the false prophets would get special attention from Micah in his rebukes?

CLEAR THE CONFUSION

What is wrong with prophets who proclaim "peace" (v. 5)?

True prophets call sinners to repent and escape God's judgment for Jesus' sake. False prophets promise God will not judge. They are like the serpent in the Garden of Eden promising Eve, "You will not surely die" (Genesis 3:4).

SET THE SCENE

Hezekiah Heeds Micah

In Jeremiah 26:18–19, we read the end result of the prophet Micah's denouncement. When Micah prophesied against Jerusalem, King Hezekiah did not put him to death but believed his message and led Judah in repentance.

The Coming of God's Salvation and His Rescue (4:1–5:15)

Micah receives a prophecy about the birthplace of the coming Messiah and His saving mission.

The Mountain of the LORD (4:1–5)

WAYPOINT

What does this text show us?
Micah prophesies Jesus' second coming to institute God's kingdom in the new heavens and the new earth on Judgment Day. All believers will gather together on God's holy mountain. Suffering, war, and hunger will be forgotten.

What does this text reveal about God's plan of salvation?
The redeemed will gather with the Lord and dwell with Him for all eternity. He alone is the one who gathers believers together and teaches them to live in peace for all eternity.

What does this text uncover about our identity and calling as God's people today?
Since we will be sinless for eternity, there will be no dissent, only joy in our lives forever. In the meantime, as we live our lives in Christ during this sinful age, we forgive one another and share this message with those around us.

How does this glorious future promised by Micah give us comfort when we see the injustice and mistreatment people suffer all around us?

What hope and comfort do you have for your future with Christ?

How can we bring healing to people in this sinful world today as we await Christ's glorious return to restore His creation?

CLEAR THE CONFUSION

What are the "latter days" (v. 1)?

The prophets often speak of the "former days" and the "latter days." The former days are the times of the Old Testament before Jesus' first coming. The latter days refer to the time between Jesus' first and second coming.

VISUALIZE

Plowshares and Pruning Hooks

In times of peace, turning the sharp edge of a sword into the tip of a plow to work the soil makes sense, just like curving a spear tip into a hook to prune fruit trees and harvest fruit. On the mountain of the Lord, there will be no need for weapons since we will all live together in peace.

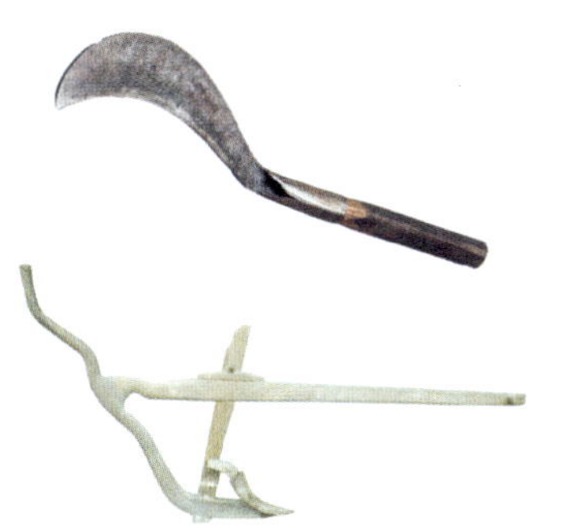

Make a mental list of the things we need to protect our families and possessions from people who would harm us (like outfitting a police department or national armed forces). What more could we do if those resources were no longer necessary?

The LORD Shall Rescue Zion (4:6–13)

The lame and weak shall be made upright and strong and enjoy God's blessings as His people. But first, Israel must endure trials and tribulations and be exiled in Babylon. Then God will favor them again.

PICTURE OF THE SAVIOR

The Lame Are Made Strong

Jesus' healing miracles fulfilled Micah's description of God strengthening the weak and needy. They give us a foretaste of the restoration He will give when He returns on Judgment Day.

The Ruler to Be Born in Bethlehem (5:1–6)

A king whose origins are from eternity will be born in Bethlehem. Jesus, the Son of God, was begotten of God the Father from eternity and conquered sin, death, and hell for us by His death and resurrection.

Why is it significant that the mighty Son of God was born in such an unimportant, out of the way, little town like Bethlehem?

VISUALIZE

Whom would you consider the remnant of the faithful in our world today?

A Remnant Shall Be Delivered (5:7–15)

Micah describes the faithful remnant of Israel, the contrite and repentant from the house of Jacob. This remnant will be raised up and God will destroy their enemies.

CLEAR THE CONFUSION

What was the remnant?

The Lord removed the faithless from among His people, leaving a remnant of faithful Jews to return to Jerusalem, rebuild the temple, and await the Messiah.

Renewed Prophecies of Doom, Ending with Restoration (6:1–7:20)

Micah closes with a warning of Judgment Day and the promise of the glorious restoration of God's creation.

The Indictment of the LORD (6:1–5)

God asks the mountains and hills to stand as silent witnesses and hear how Israel has failed in His sight. God had provided for them and delivered them from many evils, yet His people continue to rebel.

CLEAR THE CONFUSION

What happened "from Shittim to Gilgal" (v. 5)?

These were cities on the east and west banks of the Jordan River. Between the two cities, Israel fought under Joshua against greater and mightier nations as God gave the Israelites the land He had promised their fathers.

What Does the LORD Require? (6:6–8)

WAYPOINT

What does this text show us?
Micah asks what God demands of His followers. Thousands of sacrifices of livestock? Precious oil? Sacrificing a firstborn child? None of these can atone for Israel's sins. Only God can atone for our sins.

What does this text reveal about God's plan of salvation?
On our own, we are unable to fulfill the Law or pay God for our sins. We rely solely on Jesus' perfect life, sacrificial death, and glorious resurrection. He alone could fulfill all the requirements of the Law.

What does this text uncover about our identity and calling as God's people today?
God calls us to love and serve Him above all others. Since we cannot fulfill the Law on our own, we live under the grace of God. The Holy Spirit empowers us to live as the Lord's people and serve Him by serving others.

After reading this section, what are some of the ways mankind tries to justify itself?

How do the Scriptures assure you of the salvation found only in Christ?

Who do you know that needs to hear the Gospel message?

Destruction of the Wicked (6:9–16)

The wicked who profit from their deceit, cheating, and abuses shall fall victim to their own vices. They shall toil and not ever taste the fruits of their labor.

When you are overwhelmed and discouraged by the injustice, suffering, and evil around you, how does verse 7 uplift you? "But as for me, I will look to the LORD; I will wait for the God of my salvation; my God will hear me."

Wait for the God of Salvation (7:1–17)

Micah describes the entire house of Israel as evil and wicked. They constantly connive and look after their own self-interests. God will punish them and protect the righteous from their evil.

God's Steadfast Love and Compassion (7:18–20)

WAYPOINT

What does this text show us?
Although Israel now receives God's wrath, His anger will fade and He will forgive and have compassion. Even with the coming judgment, God is preparing to wipe away the sins of Israel and restore the faithful remnant of His people.

What does this text reveal about God's plan of salvation?
The Lord pardons our iniquities and casts them into the sea. This imagery brings to mind the Father's promise given in Genesis 3:15 that the Savior would crush Satan's head. Through His mercy, our sins will be removed far from us.

What does this text uncover about our identity and calling as God's people today?
God gives us reason for joy as He carries out His promises to wipe out all our sins. We can respond with joy and serve the Lord and one another. The Lord calls us to remain faithful and share His Word with others.

How does God's Word in these verses reassure you of His grace and mercy?

What promises of God do you see fulfilled in God's Word?

How can you serve the Lord in your life?

NAHUM

Welcome to Nahum

Nahum is the seventh of the twelve minor prophets. He preaches against Assyria, the enemies of God's chosen ones. Nahum depicts the sacking of Nineveh, the capital city of the Assyrian Empire. The city repented at the preaching of Jonah, approximately 150 years before, but has once again fallen into sin, mistreating the prisoners of Israel. As you read Nahum, consider Satan's age-old hatred against God and His people and rejoice at the judgment coming upon him.

Do you find it surprising that after several generations the people of Nineveh, who repented of their evil in Jonah's day, would fall back into that sin and cruelty?

Nahum at a Glance

- **Start:** Nahum reiterates parts of God's covenant with Israel and assures His wrath will be delivered in full force upon His enemies.
- **End:** Nineveh's destruction is complete, and God's people taunt the evil empire that has finally been decimated.
- **Theme:** God used Assyria to punish Israel for its disobedience. Now the Assyrians and their oppressive city are on the chopping block.
- **Author and Date:** Nahum of Elkosh records his prophetic visions sometime between the fall of Thebes in 663 BC and the destruction of Nineveh in 612 BC.
- **Places Visited:** Nineveh, situated on the Tigris River
- **Journey Time:** Nahum's three chapters take only about eight minutes to read through.
- **Outline:**
  - Reminder of the Covenant (1:1–15)
  - The Destruction and Humiliation of Nineveh (2:1–3:19)

Compare the language of Nahum with other books of poetry and prophecy. Are they similar? Different? How?

Five Top Sights and Spectacles of Nahum

The Wrath of the Lord (1:2–15) Witness Nahum's testimony regarding the power of the Lord and His character.

The Siege of Nineveh (2:1–6) Feel the desperation and fear cast in Nahum's vision of the siege and battle that would destroy Nineveh.

The Sacking of Nineveh (2:7–13) Watch as the treasures of the city are carried out and everything Nineveh once valued is looted.

The Humiliation of Nineveh (3:4–13) Observe Nineveh's humiliation: as if a prostitute, now reviled, shamed, and put on display.

Mocking the King of Assyria (3:18–19) Hearken to Nahum's final taunts at Assyria, specifically at her king.

Seeing Jesus in Nahum

Nahum shows God's wrath toward unrepentant sinners who victimize His people. We see that same wrath when Jesus drives the money-changers and sellers out of the temple (John 2:14–17). Jesus will also endure that wrath of God when He suffers in our place on the cross. We shall see this righteous judgment again when He returns to vindicate His saints against their enemies.

Reminder of the Covenant (1:1–15)

Judah trembles at the approach of the Assyrian armies. Nahum opens with a reminder that the God of Israel is a mighty warrior no nation can withstand.

Introduction (1:1)

Nahum's name means "comforter." How could his message have been a word of comfort to the Israelites?

Nahum is introduced as a prophet from Elkosh, an unknown location likely within Judah. Nahum establishes that the following writings are a God-given vision of the destruction of Nineveh.

SET THE SCENE

Oracles

Nahum's message is called an oracle. This term is used in the Bible for divinely inspired messages from God. Oracles are terrifying words of judgment from God and were most frequently spoken against the enemies of God's people.

Why is it important to see Satan, the world, and our own sinful nature as our enemies under God's wrath rather than the unbelievers around us for whom Jesus died?

God's Wrath Against Nineveh (1:2–15)

Nahum describes the extent of God's anger toward Nineveh by speaking about the destruction of mountains and oceans. He reminds Judah that this destruction will free them from the terror and yoke of the Assyrians.

SET THE SCENE

The Assyrians

Assyria was formed from a collection of Mesopotamian city-states in about 900 BC. Assyria's success in battle was fueled by skilled metalworkers who made both iron and bronze weapons. The Assyrians were renowned for their brutality and viciousness in warfare.

CLEAR THE CONFUSION

Why did Nahum switch from Law to Gospel so drastically in verse 7?

The first verses portray God's wrath toward sinners who were no longer repentant. It is important for believers to be reminded that God is good and not evil and that He is a stronghold who protects and avenges all who take refuge in Him.

The Destruction and Humiliation of Nineveh (2:1–3:19)

Nahum shifts from speaking to the people of Judah about God's deliverance to speaking to the people of Nineveh about the destruction God will bring upon their nation, Assyria.

The Destruction of Nineveh (2:1–13)

Chariots rush through Nineveh's streets, cutting down its citizens, and every precious item is seized as the city is sacked. This desolation is the work of the Lord who is against the nation of Assyria.

Nineveh Destroyed

Following a three-month siege in 612 BC, the Assyrian capital of Nineveh fell to the Babylonian armies. Assyrian King Sinsharishkun was killed during a battle. Nahum describes the battles, which included chariots, siege towers, and fierce fighting.

Woe to Nineveh (3:1–19)

Nahum concludes with a taunt at the Assyrian king, whose subjects flee, whose armies and servants are dashed apart, and whose vassals and enemies alike rejoice in his death.

What do you generally think about taunting? When might it be appropriate to taunt someone or something? How does Paul's taunting in 1 Corinthians 15:55, "O death, where is your victory? O death, where is your sting?" give us courage in the face of suffering and death?

CLEAR THE CONFUSION

What happened to Nineveh?

Following the siege of Nineveh by the Babylonians, the Assyrians briefly rallied but were finally eliminated in 608 BC. The people scattered throughout the surrounding countryside and eventually the once glorious buildings and walls became buried in the earth.

The ruins of Nineveh remained buried and lost until 1846, when archaeologists rediscovered the city and began excavating the two mounds that contained the remains of much of Nineveh. In the late twentieth century, the ruins of Nineveh were heavily vandalized, with numerous artifacts appearing on the antiquities market. Today the city of Mosul, Iraq, continues to encroach upon the historic ruins.

PICTURE OF THE SAVIOR

He Bore the Wrath of God

Nahum powerfully portrays God's wrath at the depravity and cruelty of sinful humanity. All of this fell upon Jesus when He took upon Himself the sins of the world and was crucified for us. The taunts at the end of this book remind us of the taunts and mockery Jesus endured as He hung from the cross.

HABAKKUK

Welcome to Habakkuk

Habakkuk is the eighth of the twelve minor prophets. Habakkuk records a dialogue between the prophet and the Lord, with the prophet asking where God is when evil people oppress the righteous. God teaches Habakkuk and us to trust in Him despite the wickedness all around us.

Have you ever asked yourself why God allows evil to happen? How would you answer this question if a friend asked you?

Habakkuk at a Glance

- **Start:** Habakkuk asks God why He does nothing when Jerusalem is filled with wickedness and oppression.
- **End:** Habakkuk concludes with a song of praise, rejoicing in God's love and mercy despite adverse circumstances.
- **Theme:** Despite all the evil happening around us, God promises to bring justice in His own time and in His own way.
- **Author and Date:** Habakkuk wrote this book early in Jehoiakim's reign, before the Chaldeans defeated Egypt at Carchemish, probably near 605 BC.
- **Places Visited:** Judah, Chaldea (Babylon), the watchtower, the temple
- **Journey Time:** The three chapters of Habakkuk can be read in about nine minutes.
- **Outline:**
    - The Debate Between Habakkuk and God (1:1–2:5)
    - Woes to the Arrogant (2:6–20)
    - Habakkuk's Psalm of Submission (3:1–19)

Five Top Sights and Spectacles of Habakkuk

The Complaint (1:2–4) Witness Habakkuk's frustration as he asks why God does nothing about the injustice and oppression in Judah.

Living by Faith (2:4) Listen to the Lord teach us to lean wholly on Him in faith instead of relying on human solutions.

Woes to the Oppressors (2:6–19) Hear God promise judgment against the Chaldeans for their violence, abuse, and idolatry.

The Lord in the Temple (2:20) Bask in the Lord's presence as He quiets our worries while we await His promised action.

Rejoicing in the Silence (3:17–19) Learn from Habakkuk to trust in the Lord's promises and rejoice in His faithfulness.

Seeing Jesus in Habakkuk

The Lord Jesus suffered the same injustice, oppression, and wickedness of which Habakkuk complains. On the cross, He satisfied God's wrath and won salvation for all. Although we still witness injustice and oppression, Christ will finally remove it when He returns on Judgment Day.

The Debate Between Habakkuk and God (1:1–2:5)

The prophet complains about violence in Judah and God responds. Troubled by God's answer, Habakkuk raises another complaint.

Introduction (1:1)

Habakkuk identifies himself as a prophet and his message as an oracle from God.

Habakkuk's Complaint (1:2–4)

Compare this introduction to the introduction of Job. How do Job and Habakkuk react differently to suffering and express their faith in different ways?

Judah's judges pervert justice and do not enforce the laws meant to keep wickedness in check. Habakkuk asks God why He sees yet ignores the injustice of Judah's king, nobles, priests, and merchants.

The LORD's Answer (1:5–11)

God promises to use the fearsome Chaldean army to conquer Judah, administer just vengeance, and take the Judean people into captivity.

SET THE SCENE

The Chaldeans

The Chaldeans were a tribe from the land of Babylon. Their leader, Nabopolassar, led an alliance of tribes that conquered Assyria. Nabopolassar began expanding his Babylonian empire at the time of Habakkuk. His son, Nebuchadnezzar II, would conquer Jerusalem and exile the people of Judah to Babylon.

VISUALIZE

The State of the Near East

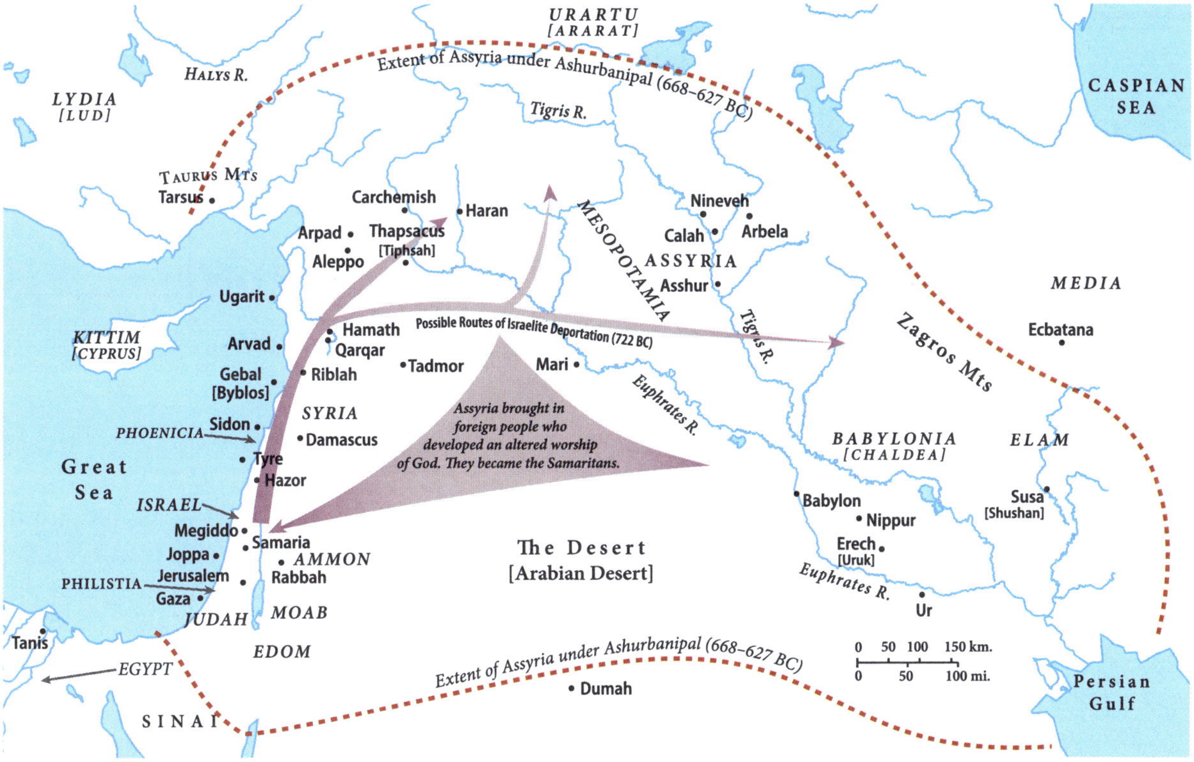

Habakkuk's Second Complaint (1:12–2:1)

Habakkuk expresses frustration that God will end Judah's wickedness through an ungodly nation. He climbs into the watchtower to await God's answer.

The Righteous Shall Live by His Faith (2:2–5)

WAYPOINT

What does this text show us?
God reassures Habakkuk that His promises are certain. He contrasts believers' trust in His promises with Babylon's trust in their own military might. God promises that Babylon's idolatry, arrogance, and greed will all incur judgment.

What does this text reveal about God's plan of salvation?
Though we live in a world ruined by sin, God is in control. Jesus Himself suffered from evil men but overcame evil, sin, and death through His own death and resurrection. On Judgment Day, He will remove all evil from His creation.

What does this text uncover about our identity and calling as God's people today?
When it seems as if God has turned away from us, we can rely on our Baptism, knowing that God will provide for us as a father provides for his children.

Read the First Commandment and its explanation in Luther's Small Catechism. What have you idolized and trusted more than God?

How did Jesus demonstrate what it means to live by faith when He was suffering on the cross?

What tools does the Holy Spirit use to deepen your trust in God's promises when it seems like He is not fulfilling them?

Woes to the Arrogant (2:6–20)

God assures Habakkuk that He will punish Babylon's wickedness and arrogance and vindicate the faithful.

Woe to the Chaldeans (2:6–20)

Habakkuk pronounces God's judgment on the Chaldeans for their greed, pride, violence, abuse, and idolatry. In these five woes, God confronts the Chaldeans with their sin and promises judgment in line with that sin.

Verse 13 speaks of how the people "labor merely for fire." How does it change your perspective on your work and possessions when you consider that Christ will destroy them all when He returns to cleanse the world with fire on Judgment Day?

CLEAR THE CONFUSION

What is "the cup in the Lord's right hand" (v. 16) that the king of the Chaldeans will have to drink?

That is God's wrath for sins. Jesus prayed about this same cup in Gethsemane, "Abba, Father, all things are possible for You. Remove this cup from Me. Yet not what I will, but what You will" (Mark 14:36). He drained this cup on the cross.

Habakkuk's Psalm of Submission (3:1–19)

Strengthened by God's promise, the prophet shares a prayer submitting to God's will in humility and trust.

Habakkuk's Prayer (3:1–16)

Habakkuk recounts God's power over peoples, nations, and all creation. He then pleads for the Lord to remember mercy and resolves himself to wait quietly for God to bring vengeance upon the Chaldeans.

Habakkuk Rejoices in the LORD (3:17–19)

VISUALIZE

How does waiting quietly show our faith in God and our trust in His promises?

How did Jesus show what it means to wait patiently as He suffered on the cross?

What can you do while you wait patiently for the new creation?

WAYPOINT

What does this text show us?

Waiting quietly for the day of God's vengeance, Habakkuk is able to rejoice in the midst of desolation. Even experiencing famine at the hands of the Chaldeans, he finds peace in God's promise to avenge and restore His people.

What does this text reveal about God's plan of salvation?

God's plan of salvation led Christ to suffer the punishment for all our sins, granting us mercy from God's wrath. As we finish our pilgrimage through this life, we trust in the certainty of God's promises, seeking Him as our strength.

What does this text uncover about our identity and calling as God's people today?

Just as God vindicated His people by destroying their oppressors, He will vindicate us as His baptized children. When we face hardships in life, we take comfort in God's promise of the new earth and live by faith in Him.

ZEPHANIAH

Welcome to Zephaniah

Zephaniah is the ninth of the twelve minor prophets. Zephaniah prophesies during the rule of righteous King Josiah and at the same time as the prophet Jeremiah. Though Josiah seeks the Lord, makes a covenant with the people, and restores proper temple worship, the people of Judah still worship at high places and dishonor God. Zephaniah supports Josiah's reforms by calling for repentance and true spiritual reform. As you read Zephaniah, lay your heart and soul bare before God. Repent of your sins and cling to Jesus Christ, your Savior and Lord.

How does it inform your reading of this book to know that God raised up Zephaniah to encourage King Josiah and strengthen his reforms?

Zephaniah at a Glance

- **Start:** The book starts with a large scale poem depicting God's wrath as being so destructive that it sweeps away His creation.
- **End:** The book ends with God promising to restore Israel and to rule as king of it and all the righteous among the nations once more.
- **Theme:** Israel resembles the wicked nations that surround it. Therefore, it shall face God's judgment just like them.
- **Author and Date:** The author is the prophet Zephaniah, who preached during the time of King Josiah between 640–609 BC.
- **Places Visited:** Jerusalem, Moab, Canaan, Ammon, Cush, Assyria, and Gaza
- **Journey Time:** It takes about ten minutes to read Zephaniah's three chapters.
- **Outline:**
  - Impending Judgment (1:1–3:8)
  - Deliverance, Restoration, and Exaltation of the Righteous (3:9–20)

What are some elements God considers to be wicked among the nations? Does your country have these sinful elements?

Five Top Sights and Spectacles of Zephaniah

Vision of Creation's Undoing (1:2–6) Witness God's power as His anger is poetically portrayed as the reversal of His creation.

Jerusalem Judged (1:10–13) Hear the cries of despair across Jerusalem. No section of the city will escape God's punishment.

Inclusion of Judah with Its Wicked Neighbors (3:1–2) See Judah swearing by false gods and perpetrating cruelty on the righteous.

The People Turn Their Hearts Toward God (3:9) Learn of God's intention to purify the wicked, pagan nations.

Israel Restored (3:16–17) Gaze upon the shining vision of a restored and holy Jerusalem.

Seeing Jesus in Zephaniah

Zephaniah warns Judah that they have fallen like the other nations, but God proclaims His mercy and promises to redeem them. Jesus is that redemption: He makes us pure in God's sight and will come again to institute God's kingdom here on Judgment Day.

Impending Judgment (1:1–3:8)

Zephaniah opens with a strong warning of judgment against Judah and the surrounding nations for their idolatry and wickedness.

Introduction (1:1)

Zephaniah preaches in the days of Josiah, who rules after two evil kings. Josiah has done much to institute religious reform but ultimately has been unable to turn the hearts of the people of Judah from their sins.

The Coming Judgment on Judah (1:2–6)

Zephaniah first warns of Judgment Day, when God will cleanse His entire creation from sin. Then, he turns back to his own time, when God will destroy Jerusalem because the people make oaths by other gods.

CLEAR THE CONFUSION

Who are the "remnant of Baal" (v. 4) and Milcom (v. 5)?

When King Josiah destroyed Molech's high places and rededicated Judah to God, many Israelites clung to their Baal worship. Milcom was another name for Molech, the Ammonite god to whom children were sacrificed.

The Day of the LORD Is Near (1:7–18)

Zephaniah declares the Lord's judgment on Israel. Every part of Jerusalem will fall, from the fish market to the upscale neighborhoods of the city.

Why are people sometimes obsessed with knowing the day of Christ's second coming? How does God reassure us about His return?

LINK BETWEEN THE TESTAMENTS

The Day of the Lord → The Coming of the Son of Man (Zephaniah 1:7–18 → Matthew 24:29–31)

Zephaniah warns the people that they will suffer distress at the hands of their enemies because of their sinfulness. Jesus describes the great tribulation and disaster which will strike the world when He returns to judge sinners.

Judgment on Judah's Enemies (2:1–15)

While most in Judah feel no shame at their sins, a few are repentant. Zephaniah urges these to seek the Lord and live in righteousness so God may spare them in the final judgment.

How does Zephaniah's call to the contrite and repentant believers among the people in Jerusalem fit well with Christians living in the midst of unbelievers today?

Judgment on Jerusalem and the Nations (3:1–8)

Zephaniah lists Judah in the company of the wicked nations he had described earlier. Jerusalem defies God and has become unrecognizable to Him. God will pour His wrath upon Jerusalem as well as its enemies.

SET THE SCENE

The Rhetoric of Entrapment

The people of Judah agreed with God's devastating judgment on the wicked people of Nineveh. When Zephaniah showed them they were just as unjust and wicked as Nineveh, they were without excuse, trapped in God's judgment.

Deliverance, Restoration, and Exaltation of the Righteous (3:9–20)

As God pours out His judgment, He will deliver the believers among His people and among the nations as He comes to dwell with His people.

The Conversion of the Nations (3:9–13)

After reading this section of Zephaniah, what questions do you have?

How did Jesus' death make it possible for God to remove evil from the world without having to remove every sinner?

How can you share God's message of forgiveness through Christ with others?

WAYPOINT

What does this text show us?
God promises to remove the haughty and wicked so only the righteous remain, who will not profane His name. There shall be no injustice, lies, mocking or evil intentions, only meekness, humility, and righteousness.

What does this text reveal about God's plan for salvation?
God's plan to cleanse the world of sin and evil includes all the nations of the earth, not just Israel itself. Jesus is the blessing through which we are saved and through which Israel was able to bless the world.

What does this text uncover about our identity and calling as God's people today?
Our identity is as forgiven children of Christ—no matter where we come from, no matter what we've done. Forgiven and purified by faith in Jesus Christ, we live in righteousness toward God and our neighbors.

Israel's Joy and Restoration (3:14–20)

God promises to restore Israel, dwell within it, and exalt it. He will quiet their fears, silence their pain, and deliver them from their oppressors.

VISUALIZE

Zephaniah's promise that the Lord would be in our midst was fulfilled in Jesus' first coming. How is it fulfilled in our lives today?

PICTURE OF THE SAVIOR

Israel's Restoring Lord

Zephaniah closes with a message of hope based on the restoration found in Christ, our Lord. The daughters of Zion will include all the Jews and Gentiles who dwell in the new Jerusalem (Hebrews 12:22).

HAGGAI

Welcome to Haggai

Haggai is the tenth of the twelve minor prophets. The final three prophets wrote after Judah returned from exile in Babylon. Reconstruction of the temple was halted because of political opposition from Judah's enemies (see Ezra 4:17–24). God raises up Haggai and Zechariah to urge the leaders to resume building and trust God while an appeal is brought to the Persian emperor. The book is sequenced over about four months. As you read Haggai, reflect on if worshiping with God's people and receiving His gifts each week is as important to you as it is to God.

How do the first six chapters of Ezra help you understand the situation Haggai is addressing and why God raised up Zechariah the prophet to join Haggai in encouraging the Judeans to rebuild the temple?

Haggai at a Glance

- **Start:** The book starts with Haggai telling the people not to neglect the temple in their reconstruction of the city.
- **End:** Haggai ends with God's promise to send the Messiah through the line of David and, consequently, from Zerubbabel's descendants.
- **Theme:** The people of Israel have become focused on their own lives and have to relearn what it is to live as a nation under God.
- **Author and Date:** The prophet Haggai wrote the book in 520 BC, when the Israelites returned from exile.
- **Places Visited:** Jerusalem
- **Journey Time:** It takes about seven minutes to read the two chapters of Haggai.
- **Outline:**
  - The Command to Rebuild the Temple (1:1–15)
  - The Coming Glory of the Temple (2:1–23)

Five Top Sights and Spectacles of Haggai

God Demands the Temple Be Rebuilt (1:7–9) Watch God warn the people about neglecting His temple as they reconstruct their homes.

The People Listen to God (1:14) Marvel as God empowers the people to resume their work on the temple at Haggai's urging.

Vision of the Temple's Coming Glory (2:9) Listen in wonder as Haggai promises this temple will surpass Solomon's glorious temple.

God Promises to Cleanse His People (2:14–16) See the futility of building our lives without putting God first.

God Promises Zerubbabel's Lineage Will Bear the Sign of His Salvation (2:23) Hear God renew His promise to send the Savior from the house of David through the descendants of Zerubbabel.

Seeing Jesus in Haggai

Jesus is seen in God's promise to bless His people despite their unclean state. Jesus does this through His sacrifice, purifying Israel's sins and those of the entire world. At the end of the book God promises to make Zerubbabel like a signet. Zerubbabel sets the future for the line of David, from which God will bring Christ into the world.

The Command to Rebuild the Temple (1:1–15)

Haggai records the Lord's command to resume rebuilding the temple and the obedience of the returned exiles.

The Command to Rebuild the Temple (1:1–11)

Haggai confronts Zerubbabel the governor and Joshua the priest about neglecting the temple. The people who returned to Judah have endured hardship with famine, drought, and scarcity because they have looked after themselves first and rejected rebuilding God's temple.

Consider how much of your time and finances you contribute to the work of your congregation compared to what you invest in your family and home. What can you learn from Haggai's word to these two Judean leaders?

CLEAR THE CONFUSION

Why had the people neglected rebuilding the temple?

When the temple reconstruction was forcibly halted under order of the Persian king, the Judeans and their leaders turned their focus on building their own private homes instead of rebuilding the temple.

The People Obey the LORD (1:12–15)

After Haggai's preaching, Zerubbabel and Joshua heed God's word. Stirred by the Holy Spirit, they lead the remnant of the people to turn their hearts toward God and resume restoring and rebuilding the temple.

Who encourages you to heed God's Word in your life?

SET THE SCENE

The Hidden Risk of Rebuilding the Temple

The last official word from the king of Persia was that the work on the temple must cease and the city not be rebuilt (Ezra 4:17–24). It took faith in God's word for Zerubbabel and Joshua to renew construction and place their names on the governor's letter to King Darius.

The Coming Glory of the Temple (2:1–23)

The Lord promises this temple will be even more glorious than Solomon's temple because the Messiah will stand in its courts.

The Coming Glory of the Temple (2:1–9)

Three-and-a-half weeks later, the Lord calls Haggai to encourage Zerubbabel and Joshua once more. God promises to exalt this temple and foretells that all the nations will bring their treasures to the temple.

The Israelites anxiously anticipated the restoration of the temple. What are you anxiously awaiting?

VISUALIZE

CLEAR THE CONFUSION

What did God mean when He said the "latter glory of this house" would be greater than the former glory (v. 9)?

Jesus Christ would come to this very temple and teach and work miracles in its courts. The presence of God Incarnate made this temple more glorious than Solomon's temple.

How would you describe the appearance of your church building? How does Christ's presence in Word and Sacrament make it more glorious than an empty cathedral?

PICTURE OF THE SAVIOR

Jesus, Our Living Temple

During Jesus' trial, the chief priests twisted His statement about rebuilding the temple in three days (see Matthew 26:61; 27:40, 63) into a threat to destroy it. But Jesus referred to His body, which He would raise on the third day.

When Jesus became incarnate, the fullness of His deity dwelt within His human body, in which He came and dwelt among us as God's temple. How are you and all believers temples of God now?

Blessings for a Defiled People (2:10–19)

Haggai points out that the returned exiles are unclean because they have stopped rebuilding the temple. God promises to bless them from the day they return to rebuilding the temple and restoring its proper service.

Zerubbabel Chosen as a Signet (2:20–23)

Haggai speaks directly to the governor Zerubbabel. He reiterates God's promise to bless all the world through Zerubbabel, a descendant of David. The Messiah will come as God had promised long ago.

What faithful leaders has God provided for you in your everyday life?

CLEAR THE CONFUSION

What is a signet ring?

A signet ring was engraved with a person's name or symbol and used to authenticate documents and seals. It could be entrusted to a high official who ruled in the name and authority of that ruler (see Esther 8:2).

ZECHARIAH

Welcome to Zechariah

Zechariah is the eleventh of the twelve minor prophets. Two months after sending Haggai, God sends Zechariah to reinforce His message to rebuild the temple. Zechariah offers numerous messianic prophecies focused on Holy Week events. As you read Zechariah, take comfort in the knowledge that Jesus took your sins upon Himself as He died on the cross, and He gives you His own righteousness and peace.

The temple was the only place where Jews could offer sacrifices and atone for their sins. If your church was destroyed and there was no other place to hear God's Word and receive His Sacraments, how big of a priority would it be for you to rebuild your sanctuary as quickly as possible?

Zechariah at a Glance

- **Start:** Zechariah begins with a call to the exiles to repent and not be like their stubborn ancestors.
- **End:** Zechariah ends with a vision of Judgment Day and the eternal age when believers live in glory with Christ forever.
- **Theme:** Zechariah encourages the returned exiles to rebuild the temple and prophesies the final week of Christ's ministry.
- **Author and Date:** Zechariah wrote this book during the reign of the Persian king Darius. This occurred between 520–518 BC.
- **Places Visited:** Judah, Jerusalem, Zion, the temple, the Mount of Olives, and surrounding nations
- **Journey Time:** The fourteen chapters of Zechariah can be read in about forty minutes.
- **Outline:**
  - Introductory Oracle and "Night Visions" (1:1–6:8)
  - The Coming Peace and Prosperity (6:9–10:12)
  - Holy Week Prophecies (11:1–13:9)
  - Varied Pictures of the Last Day (14:1–21)

Five Top Sights and Spectacles of Zechariah

A Series of Visions (1:7–6:8) See the eight visions God gives to remind the Judeans of His power and the importance of the temple.

Coronation of Priest and King (6:9–15) Celebrate as Zechariah crowns Joshua high priest and prophesies about the coming Messiah.

The Victorious King (9:9–13) Rejoice with the daughters of Zion as you behold the Messiah entering Jerusalem in triumph.

The Shepherd Zechariah (11:4–17) Experience a shepherd's life as God calls Zechariah to shepherd a flock doomed for slaughter.

The Wounded Shepherd (13:7–9) Witness God striking His trusted shepherd, pointing forward to Christ's death for us on the cross.

Seeing Jesus in Zechariah

Zechariah contains more prophecies of Holy Week events than any other Old Testament book. Zechariah emphasizes Jesus' role in our lives as Priest, King, and Shepherd.

Introductory Oracle and "Night Visions" (1:1–6:8)

Zechariah opens with a call from the Lord to His people and eight visions that reveal God's gracious purposes for His people.

When we repent, how do our new actions show that we have returned to God?

Have you ever interceded for someone or mediated a conflict between two people? Do you think it would be easy to convince a friend to completely forgive someone who has deeply hurt him or her?

A Call to Return to the LORD (1:1–6)

Zechariah calls Judah to listen to God's Word, unlike their fathers who stubbornly refused, which resulted in the destruction of Solomon's temple and the exile. These Judeans repent and are prepared to obey God.

A Vision of a Horseman (1:7–17)

God begins showing Zechariah a series of visions in the night. The first vision depicts a horseman speaking with God as God announces His return to Jerusalem and the reconstruction of the temple.

PICTURE OF THE SAVIOR

The Man Among the Myrtle Trees

The man among the myrtle trees is the first of many depictions in Zechariah of the preincarnate Christ. Christ intercedes for Jerusalem, asking the Father to relent from His wrath and have mercy upon the people of Judah.

A Vision of Horns and Craftsmen (1:18–21)

God shows Zechariah a vision of four horns, representing the nations who have oppressed and defeated God's people. God commands four craftsmen to subdue these evil nations and protect God's people.

A Vision of a Man with a Measuring Line (2:1–13)

God shows Zechariah a vision in which a man goes out to measure Jerusalem. When Christ comes, Zion's vast population will extend far beyond Jerusalem's walls. God will protect His church.

What is the largest city you have ever visited? Can you imagine a city that is ten times that size?

CLEAR THE CONFUSION

Why did God urge His people, still scattered in the north and dwelling with the daughter of Babylon, to flee and escape to Zion (vv. 6–7)?

When the exiles were permitted to return to Jerusalem, only a small number actually left Babylon. Those who stayed risked losing their faith by living among unbelievers and not joining fellow believers in God's holy temple.

A Vision of Joshua the High Priest (3:1–10)

In the fourth vision, Satan stands before God, ready to accuse Joshua, the high priest of Judah. But God cuts off Satan's accusation and rebukes him. The Lord replaces Joshua's soiled vestments with pure vestments.

How does God give you clear reminders of His forgiveness, especially when your sin and guilt weigh heavily on you?

CLEAR THE CONFUSION

What day was God promising when He said, "I will remove the iniquity of this land in a single day" (v. 9)?

God pointed ahead to Good Friday, when Christ Jesus, the faithful High Priest, would pay the punishment for the sins of all people on the cross in a single day.

A Vision of a Golden Lampstand (4:1–14)

An angel rouses Zechariah and begins a series of four more visions. The first vision depicts the eyes of God, the high priest, and the appointed governor of Judah watching over the reconstruction of the temple.

LINK BETWEEN THE TESTAMENTS

Golden Lampstand → Seven Lampstands (Zechariah 4:1–14 → Revelation 1:9–16)

Christ dwells in the midst of His church. In Revelation 1, John received a vision of Jesus standing in the middle of seven lampstands. He announced that the seven lampstands are the seven churches to whom John addresses his letters.

Why do you think God is extra concerned about thieves and perjurers?

A Vision of a Flying Scroll (5:1–4)

Zechariah receives another vision, depicting a massive flying scroll that contains God's curses for all who steal and lie. The Lord declares that He will send this curse out to pursue thieves and perjurers.

A Vision of a Woman in a Basket (5:5–11)

In another vision, the woman, Wickedness, is inside a basket being carried off by angel-like women from Jerusalem to Shinar, where the Babylonians would build a temple for idolatry.

CLEAR THE CONFUSION

What did the basket being carried from Jerusalem to Babylon signify?

Idolatry was the chief sin that led to the destruction of Jerusalem and the temple and to the exile of the people of Judah. God was reminding the exiles who had returned to Judah that idolatry no longer had a place in their lives.

Compare this vision to the first vision in 1:7–17. How are these visions similar? How are they different? How do these details shape the message of each vision?

A Vision of Four Chariots (6:1–8)

In Zechariah's final vision, four chariots leave from two bronze mountains out to the four winds of heaven, bringing the power of God against Judah's enemies so the Spirit can bring peace to God's people.

The Coming Peace and Prosperity (6:9–10:12)

The Lord promises to bless His people, establish justice, and bring peace and prosperity through the coming Savior.

The Crown and the Temple (6:9–15)

Zechariah delivers a message from God to Joshua, the high priest. He makes a crown and places it on Joshua's head, choosing him to rebuild the temple. Then Zechariah prophesies more about the Messiah.

A Call for Justice and Mercy (7:1–14)

A delegation from Bethel asks the priests if they can stop the fasting they have done through the seventy years of exile. Zechariah commands them to repent of their sin of selfish fasting, speak truth, and act justly.

The Coming Peace and Prosperity of Zion (8:1–23)

God depicts the transformation Jerusalem will experience now that He has returned to His people. He promises peace, abundant harvests, and cities full of people, both young and old.

Judgment on Israel's Enemies (9:1–8)

God continues to encourage Judah, promising judgment on the cities and nations that historically have stood in opposition to His people. He promises to come among them and protect them with His mighty power.

Why do you think this judgment was so comforting to the people of Judah?

The Coming King of Zion (9:9–13)

VISUALIZE

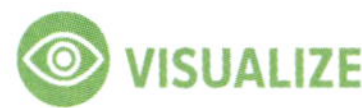

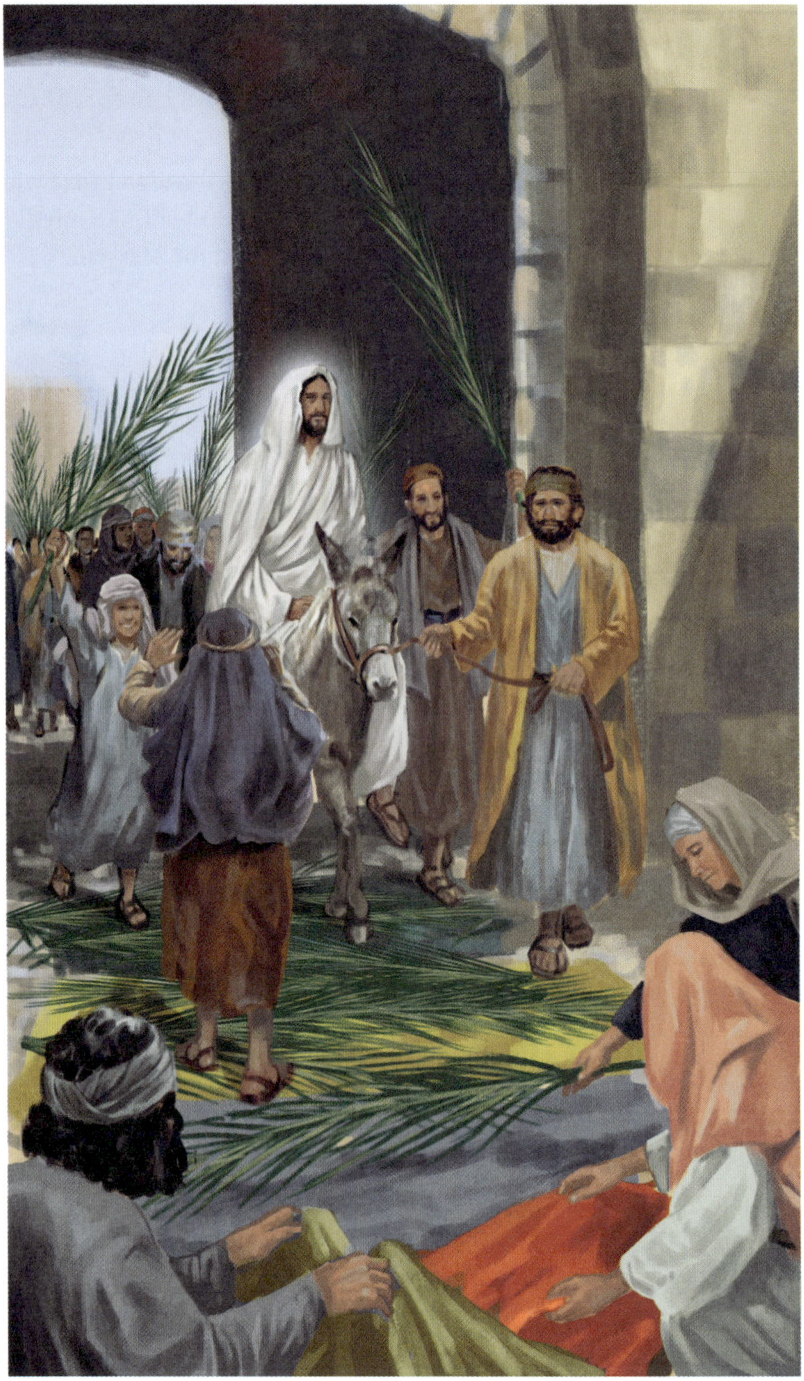

WAYPOINT

What does this text show us?
Zechariah describes the Messiah riding into Jerusalem in victory, prefiguring Palm Sunday, when Christ enters Jerusalem to conquer Satan by His death on the cross. On the Last Day, He will return in glory to eternally destroy Satan.

What does this text reveal about God's plan of salvation?
Jesus Christ fulfills all of God's promises while keeping the Law perfectly. As we read vivid promises throughout the Old Testament, we can witness the fulfillment of those promises through Christ in the New Testament.

What does this text uncover about our identity and calling as God's people today?
As we witness Christ's fulfillment of God's promises, God builds a bond of trust as we have faith that He keeps His Word. This roots our identity in God's promises, allowing us to lean on them for comfort throughout our earthly lives.

Do you ever think of Jesus as a powerful warrior? What special nuance and comfort does that offer compared to picturing Jesus as the Good Shepherd?

In deep humility, Jesus received the praises of the crowds. Why is it fitting for us to praise His willingness to go to the cross for us?

Why is it important for God to show us pictures of Jesus and promise us salvation?

LINK BETWEEN THE TESTAMENTS

Daughter of Zion (Zechariah 9:9 → Matthew 21:5)

Jesus fulfilled this prophecy when He rode into Jerusalem on the Sunday before His death. Many events of Jesus' last week, called Holy Week, will be prophesied in the coming chapters of Zechariah and fulfilled perfectly by Jesus.

The LORD Will Save His People (9:14–17)

God stands over His people as a mighty warrior who protects and saves His people, destroying all His enemies and allowing His people to flourish. God describes His people like a flock and jewels in a crown.

The Restoration for Judah and Israel (10:1–12)

God will punish those who led Israel and Judah away from Him, but He will restore His people and bless them. God returns His people to the Promised Land from their exiles in Egypt and Assyria.

Why do you think God chose to deliver Israel and Judah from the nations with the strongest militaries?

LINK BETWEEN THE TESTAMENTS

Wandering Sheep (Zechariah 10:2 → Matthew 9:36)

God noted that the people of Israel, misled by their false prophets, wandered like sheep without a shepherd. Therefore, God would destroy the false shepherds. During His public ministry, Jesus noted the great crowds were like sheep without a shepherd and was filled with compassion for them.

Holy Week Prophecies (11:1–13:9)

Zechariah gives the most detailed prophecies of Jesus' last week, including His triumphal entry, betrayal by Judas, and crucifixion.

The Flock Doomed to Slaughter (11:1–17)

God calls Zechariah to shepherd a flock of sheep who are doomed to be slaughtered. God warns that, just as in the past, more worthless leaders will rise in the future trying to lead God's people astray.

LINK BETWEEN THE TESTAMENTS

Thirty Pieces of Silver (Zechariah 11:12–13 → Matthew 26:15; 27:3–10)

When Zechariah abandoned his flock and sold them, the sheep traders paid him thirty pieces of silver. At God's command, Zechariah took these wages to the temple and cast them to the potter.

Judas Iscariot betrayed Jesus for thirty pieces of silver. Feeling deep remorse when he knew Jesus was condemned, Judas cast the money into the temple and hanged himself. The chief priests used this blood money to buy a potter's field to bury strangers.

The LORD Will Give Salvation (12:1–9)

WAYPOINT

What does this text show us?
God will strengthen Judah, making it a formidable military force. He will strengthen Jerusalem to be an unconquerable city, and Judah will go out and conquer the surrounding nations, reestablishing Judah's glory.

What does this text reveal about God's plan of salvation?
God uses weak things to destroy the arrogant. Tiny Israel conquered the Promised Land by God's strength. God's greatest victory over sin, death, and the devil was won by a beaten, bloody Christ dying on the cross.

How does Judah's worldly weakness reveal God's power and amplify His strength?

Why does it require humility and faith to trust that Jesus' death on the cross defeated Satan, sin, death, and hell?

What does this text uncover about our identity and calling as God's people today?
Although we may feel inadequate to face the trials ahead of us, we take comfort in God's strength that He will work through us. However, we are also called to recognize God's power and give Him the glory.

How does God compensate for your weaknesses when He works through you?

Him Whom They Have Pierced (12:10–13:1)

The people of Judah recognize their sin and mourn the death of God's only Son, the Messiah. The fountain in 13:1 is the wound in Jesus' side where the Roman soldier will thrust his spear to prove Jesus is dead.

PICTURE OF THE SAVIOR

The Pierced King

As we gaze upon the effect—that is, the brutal death of God's only Son—of our wicked deeds, we should repent and ask God for forgiveness. Christ was pierced by the nails and spear in our place, making atonement for all people.

Idolatry Cut Off (13:2–6)

God will remove the names of idols, false prophets, and the unclean spirits from the land. The people will enforce God's Law, with parents and friends remaining loyal to God above their children and friends.

Why was God's response—cutting off idols and false prophets—a fitting response to Judah's repentance? Why is it necessary for God to cut off our false gods?

The Shepherd Struck (13:7–9)

God turns His sword against His own servant, striking Him and scattering all of His sheep. Most of the sheep will die, and the remaining sheep will suffer, but they will be faithful to God.

PICTURE OF THE SAVIOR

The Good Shepherd Is Struck

When God turned His wrath against Jesus, all of His disciples fled and the crowds called for His crucifixion. Jesus purchased us through His blood so that we are His people and He is our God.

Varied Pictures of the Last Day (14:1–21)

Zechariah discusses the Last Day, when God will judge all nations.

Compare other examples of this vivid imagery, such as Ezekiel 38–39 and Revelation 12:7–17. What do all of these passages describe? Why does God consistently use such vivid and violent imagery for that purpose?

The Coming Day of the LORD (14:1–21)

Zechariah gives a vivid prophecy of the Last Day, when God will vindicate Jerusalem and bring vengeance on the nations. God will destroy the surrounding armies with His divine might and restore Jerusalem forever.

CLEAR THE CONFUSION

When will God gather the nations to fight against Jerusalem?

This same battle, known as Armageddon (Revelation 16:16), is discussed in Ezekiel 38 and Revelation 20. It indicates a conflict between the nations and the church that will come at the time of Christ's return on Judgment Day.

LINK BETWEEN THE TESTAMENTS

Jerusalem's Living Water → The River of Life (Zechariah 14:8 → Revelation 22:1–5)

In both Zechariah and Revelation, God shows us Jerusalem with living water flowing from it. Living water is an image of running water, which sustains the city and does not breed algae and bacteria the way stagnant water does.

MALACHI

Welcome to Malachi

Malachi is the last book of the Old Testament, written eighty years after the temple had been rebuilt and sacrifices restored. The people of Judah still withhold their love from God by offering blemished sacrifices and refusing to tithe. God reassures Judah of His love as He promises to send the Messiah and His messenger, John the Baptist, who will go in the spirit of Elijah to prepare the people for their Savior's coming. As you read Malachi, consider again God's offer of peace, salvation, and eternal life as you anticipate the return of Jesus Christ to judge the living and the dead.

What do you know of Malachi? What do you hope to learn from this book?

Malachi at a Glance

- **Start:** Malachi declares God's love for Judah by promising to oppose Israel's perpetual enemy, Edom.
- **End:** God promises to send the prophet Elijah to prepare the Messiah's way by turning people's hearts toward one another.
- **Theme:** God loves Judah and will show that love through His Messiah despite their unfaithfulness to God and one another.
- **Author and Date:** *Malachi* means "my messenger." Malachi preached during Nehemiah's second term as governor of Judah.
- **Places Visited:** Judah, Edom, and the Lord's altar
- **Journey Time:** The four chapters of Malachi can be read in about eleven minutes.
- **Outline:**
  - Correction for the Priests (1:1–2:9)
  - The People Must Be Faithful Through Proper Marriage Practice (2:10–3:5)
  - A Call to Return to the Lord in Repentance (3:6–4:6)

Five Top Sights and Spectacles of Malachi

Wastelands of Edom (1:2–5) Behold God's love for Israel as He makes Edom an uninhabitable wasteland.

Polluted Sacrifices (1:6–14) Witness the audacity of the priests who sacrifice disabled animals, denying God His honor.

Garments of Violence (2:14–16) Hear the Lord's accusation against the Judeans who have divorced their wives and married foreigners.

Refiner's Fire and Fullers' Soap (3:1–4) Smell the lye of the soap as God sends His messenger to purify Judah.

Robbing God (3:6–15) Experience the Lord's disappointment as His people refuse to tithe to support God's priests and Levites.

Seeing Jesus in Malachi

Jesus is discussed expressly in chapter 3 as the prophet predicts His appearance at the temple recently rebuilt. By Jesus' death and resurrection, He purifies us, erasing the stain of our sin and allowing us to stand before God in His righteousness on the Last Day.

Correction for the Priests (1:1–2:9)

God confronts abuses from the priests that have defiled the temple worship.

Introduction (1:1)

Malachi presents his prophetic credentials: he is a messenger who was given an oracle from God to deliver to Israel.

The LORD's Love for Israel (1:2–5)

What situations in life can make Christians question if God really loves them or not?

After Judah questions God's love, God discusses how He judged Esau's descendants, the Edomites. The Babylonians left the land of Edom uninhabitable, while God had restored the land of Judah.

CLEAR THE CONFUSION

Did God hate Esau?

Truly, God hates no one whom He has made. But His wrath does fall upon those who persistently reject Him and oppress His beloved believers. That is what Edom (Esau's descendants) had done through the generations.

The Priests' Polluted Offerings (1:6–14)

God rebukes the priests for accepting and offering blind, lame, and sick animals when the greedy Judeans had pure animals available to sacrifice to the Lord.

Imagine if God looked at our worship and said, "Oh that there were one among you who would shut the doors" (v. 10). What would make our worship unacceptable and offensive to God?

SET THE SCENE

The Jewish Sacrificial System

The first seven chapters of Leviticus established the rules for Israel's sacrifices. Only unblemished animals were permissible. Israel cheapened God's holiness by attempting to purify themselves with impure sacrifices.

The LORD Rebukes the Priests (2:1–9)

God proclaims His curse on the Jewish priests because they have forsaken His covenant with the priesthood. He accuses the priests of leading the people of Judah into sin by setting a poor example in their own lives.

Besides their role as teachers, why is it important for religious leaders to live a righteous life?

The People Must Be Faithful Through Proper Marriage Practice (2:10–3:5)

God confronts exiles who divorced their wives and married foreign women.

Judah Profaned the Covenant (2:10–16)

WAYPOINT

What does this text show us?
Malachi addresses Judean men who divorced their wives to marry foreign women. God views marriage as a sacred covenant, and He despises when Judah turns away from this covenant, harming their spouses and children.

What was so dangerous about Judean men marrying foreign women in the centuries before Christ's first coming?

In what ways is God's plan for marriage countercultural in our world?

What challenges do you face in living up to God's plan for marriage and family?

What does this text reveal about God's plan of salvation?
God designed marriage to illustrate the eternal relationship between Christ and His church. When Adam and Eve were unfaithful to God in the Garden, Jesus did not divorce them but gave His life to win their forgiveness.

What does this text uncover about our identity and calling as God's people today?
God rebukes the broader population of Judah for breaking His covenant with them, breaking their marriage vows through divorce, and marrying pagan wives. He calls us to follow His plan for our lives.

The Messenger of the LORD (2:17–3:5)

WAYPOINT

What does this text show us?
Although God expresses His displeasure with Judah's offerings, He promises to come in the person of the Messiah to make Judah's sacrifices pleasing and to restore God's people to a proper relationship with Him.

What does this text reveal about God's plan of salvation?
Jesus Christ lived a perfect life and died for our sins to provide us with His righteousness, which we need to be pure and presentable before God. Christ will come again on the Last Day to judge the living and the dead.

What does this text uncover about our identity and calling as God's people today?
Our identity as God's people does not depend on our own righteousness but on Christ's atoning death on the cross. As the purified people of God, we are now called to be living sacrifices, sharing the Gospel with our neighbors.

Why was God displeased with Judah's offerings when He had commanded them?

How can you thank God for giving you Christ as the source of your righteousness?

What sacrifices of time, talents, and treasures do you give as part of your Christian life?

CLEAR THE CONFUSION

What are a refiner's fire and fullers' soap (3:2)?

Refiners used fire to melt precious metals like silver to separate the worthless materials from the pure metal. Fullers washed woolen garments with strong soaps made of lye. Jesus makes us pure and holy through His blood.

PICTURE OF THE SAVIOR

The Messenger and the Lord

God promised to send a messenger to prepare the way before the Christ. John the Baptist prepared the way for Jesus Christ to come to the temple and purify Judah from their sins.

A Call to Return to the Lord in Repentance (3:6–4:6)

God calls the people of Jerusalem to return to Him, as He will soon send the promised Messiah.

We are no longer obligated to tithe, so how do you determine how much you will give to your church?

Robbing God (3:6–15)

God reminds the people of His steadfast love and mercy, but He levels another charge at the people of Judah for robbing Him by refusing to tithe and expecting Him to overlook their sin.

The Book of Remembrance (3:16–18)

Many refuse to tithe because they think God will not treat them any differently from those who do tithe. But some people of Judah heed His word and repent from the heart. God promises to spare them.

LINK BETWEEN THE TESTAMENTS

The Book of Remembrance → The Book of Life (Malachi 3:16–18 → Revelation 21:27)

Malachi speaks of God recording those who repent and serve Him in a book of remembrance so that He might spare them on the Last Day. Revelation speaks of the Book of Life, which records those who believe in Jesus.

Most books of the Bible point us to Christ's return on Judgment Day. Why is it important to be mindful of that day as we live our daily lives?

The Great Day of the LORD (4:1–6)

Malachi closes out his book with a warning about Judgment Day. On that day, God will punish the wicked and vindicate the righteous.

SET THE SCENE

Hark! The Herald Angels Sing

In the third stanza of "Hark! The Herald Angels Sing" (*LSB* 380), the text refers to Malachi 4:2: "The sun of righteousness shall rise with healing in its wings." This Christmas hymn points ahead to Judgment Day, when Christ will rise like the morning sun and heal us of all our sins and bodily afflictions and we will live before Him in purity and truth forevermore.

When we sing Christmas carols and hymns, why is it fitting to think of Jesus' return on Judgment Day to restore His creation and raise us to eternal life?